Jo Verso's
CROSS STITCH GIFTS FOR CHILDREN

Lord look upon a little child
By nature sinful, rude and wild,
O lay thy gracious hand on me
And make me all I aught to be.

(Caroline Mason, aged 10, 1887)

Jo Verso's
CROSS STITCH GIFTS FOR CHILDREN

David & Charles

To my sister, Antoinette

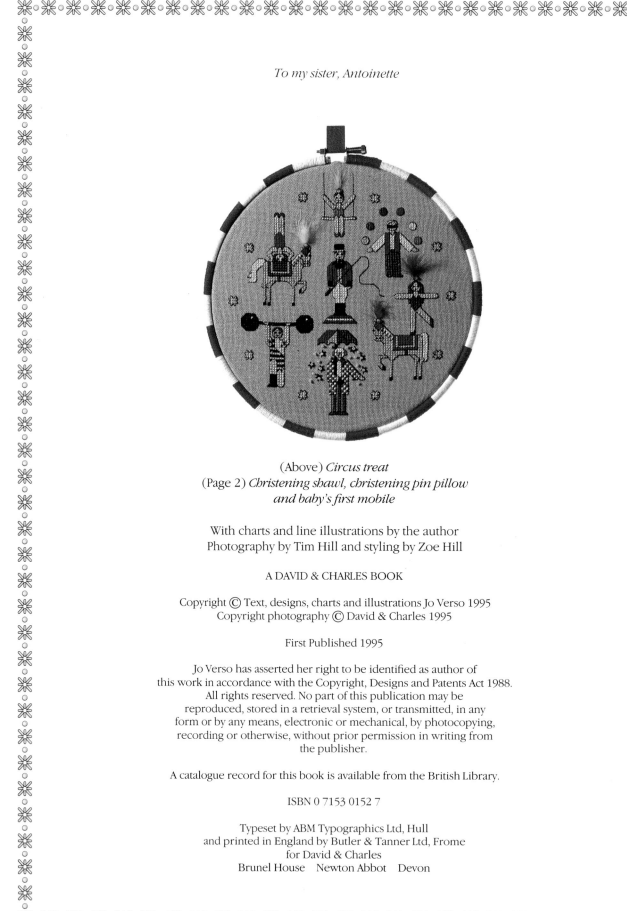

(Above) *Circus treat*
(Page 2) *Christening shawl, christening pin pillow
and baby's first mobile*

With charts and line illustrations by the author
Photography by Tim Hill and styling by Zoe Hill

A DAVID & CHARLES BOOK

Typeset by ABM Typographics Ltd, Hull
and printed in England by Butler & Tanner Ltd, Frome
for David & Charles
Brunel House   Newton Abbot   Devon

Contents

Introduction

Cross stitch embroidery was familiar to children in previous centuries mainly in the form of cross stitch samplers. School children would painstakingly stitch a sampler as a classroom exercise which taught them much more than just the skills of needlework. Several styles of alphabet were generally worked to teach literacy, and frequently a verse of high moral tone would be included. The latter served to instil piety and respect for their elders into the children.

Nowadays cross stitch has become a popular and increasingly absorbing pastime providing hours of pleasure to adults and children alike. To bring the joy of cross stitch even closer to children, I have designed these keepsakes which youngsters will be delighted to receive from the adults in their lives. Many of the projects are simple enough for children to stitch themselves, the emphasis being on fun, both for the stitcher and the recipient.

Starting with a card to welcome a new baby and progressing through all the stages of childhood, you will find a gift for most occasions here.

Each project is graded with butterfly symbols to denote the level of stitching skill required to work the design: the fewer butterflies, the simpler the task. Projects are accompanied by helpful tips provided from actual experience of either stitching or mounting the embroidery. The finished size of each piece is given to the nearest ¼in (5mm). This denotes the size of the embroidery, not the frame, mount or finished project. Full instructions are given for the stitching, mounting or finishing of the work to ensure that your projects are a complete success.

The designs in this book can be supplemented with patterns from my previous three books, *Picture It in Cross Stitch*, *Cross Stitch Cards and Keepsakes* and *Jo Verso's World of Cross Stitch*.

The picture opposite shows a record of the milestones in my elder daughter's childhood. Designs have been taken from my previous books and have been adapted to show her progress. This

(Above) Author aged 3; (opposite) Milestones

design is limited to twelve events, but a much more complete record can be made from birth right up to marriage if you so wish. Throughout my books you will find many figures which can be adapted to suit the circumstances to produce a unique and nostalgic picture of childhood progress.

Those of you who do not want to undertake your own designs will find that the patterns in this book can be stitched straight off the page without any alteration. Some designs will become more personal if you add details such as names and dates, so alphabets and numbers are supplied to enable you to do this.

It is my hope that you and the children in your life will derive as much pleasure from these projects as I have had from producing them. Childhood is fleeting and your cross stitch gifts will last long into the adulthood of those who receive them. With luck, they may be so treasured that they are handed down to the next generation.

To Welcome a New Baby

Nothing makes me reach for my needle more than the arrival of a new baby. This design is presented in three colourways and can be sent either to the baby or to the proud parents. An alphabet and numbers are provided so that you can personalise the card with the baby's name and birth date. The mauve version can be stitched in advance of the birth so that you just need to add the name and date after the baby's arrival. Ribbon, lace and Algerian eyelets are incorporated into the design to give a delicate appearance to the card.

FINISHED SIZE 3¼ x 3¼in (8.5 x 8.5cm)

YOU WILL NEED:
6 x 6in (15 x 15cm) 18 count Aida fabric, colour 264/cream
Stranded cottons (floss) as in the colour key
Tapestry needle, size 26
6in (15cm) ribbon, 1.5mm (¹⁄₁₆in) wide
8in (20cm) lace, ¼in (5mm) wide
Card mount with a 3¼in (8.5cm) diameter window
Trimmings of your choice
UHU glue

Use 2 strands of stranded cotton (floss) to work all cross stitches. Work back stitches, couching stitches (Fig 1), and Algerian eyelets (Fig 2) with one strand.

When the embroidery is complete, mount it into a card following the instructions on page 117. Trim the card by glueing lace around the window, or add other trimmings of your choice.

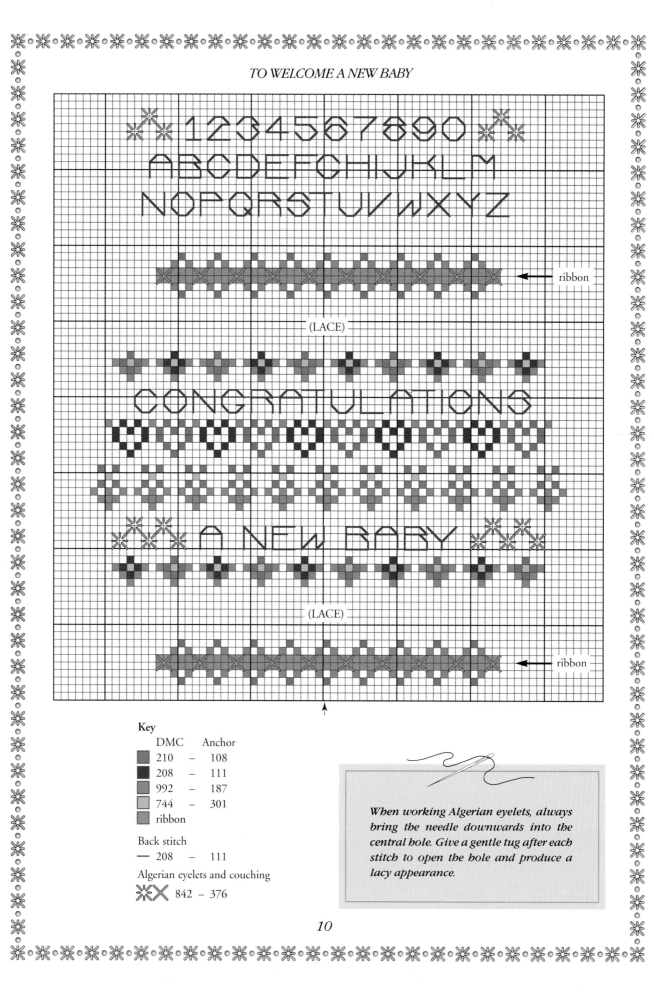

← ribbon

(LACE)

1234567890
ABCDEFGHIJKLM
NOPQRSTUVWXYZ

CONGRATULATIONS

A NEW BABY

(LACE)

← ribbon

Key

DMC		Anchor
210	–	108
208	–	111
992	–	187
744	–	301
ribbon		

Back stitch
— 208 – 111

Algerian eyelets and couching
✳✕ 842 – 376

When working Algerian eyelets, always bring the needle downwards into the central hole. Give a gentle tug after each stitch to open the hole and produce a lacy appearance.

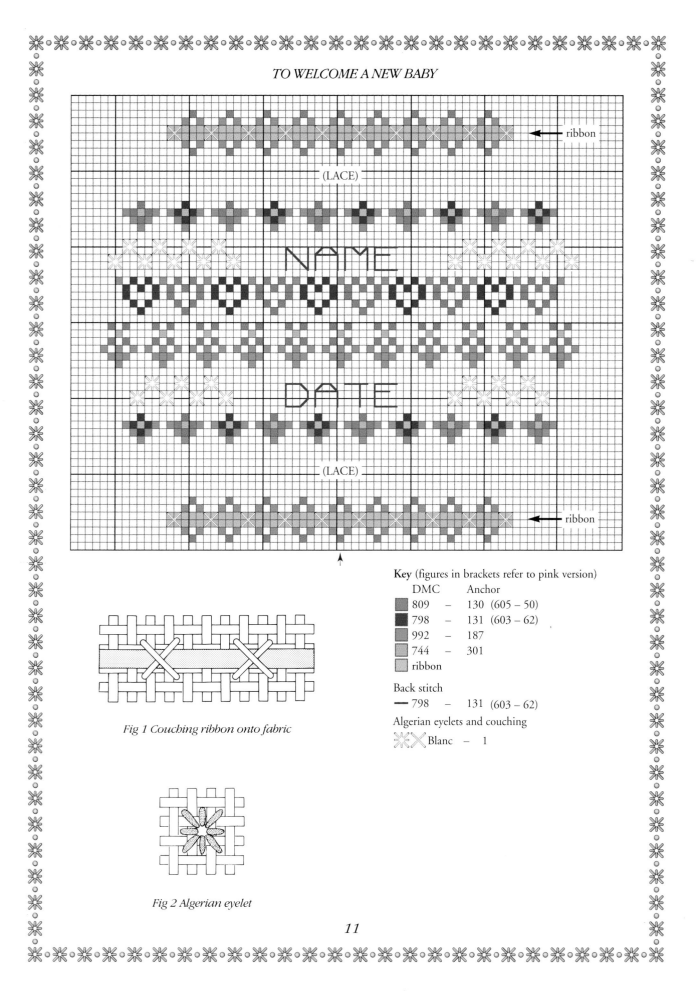

ribbon

(LACE)

NAME

DATE

(LACE)

ribbon

Fig 1 Couching ribbon onto fabric

Key (figures in brackets refer to pink version)

DMC		Anchor
809	–	130 (605 – 50)
798	–	131 (603 – 62)
992	–	187
744	–	301
ribbon		

Back stitch

— 798 – 131 (603 – 62)

Algerian eyelets and couching

Blanc – 1

Fig 2 Algerian eyelet

Birth Record

The stork was out on another call, so this baby baled out and found a novel method of delivery.
Use this design to record for posterity the birth details of a new baby. Add the name, date, time and weight using the alphabet and numbers provided. Omit the flowers at the top if you are using a longer name.

FINISHED SIZE 4¼ x 6in (11 x 15cm)

YOU WILL NEED:
10 x 12in (26 x 31cm) Zweigart Linda fabric, colour 264/ivory
Stranded cottons (floss) as in the colour key
Tapestry needle, size 26
Graph paper
Frame

Use 2 strands of stranded cotton (floss) to work all cross stitches. Work back stitches and French knots with 1 strand.

To add the name and other details, use the alphabet and numbers provided.

1 Copy out the top border onto a sheet of graph paper.
2 Draw out the name onto another slip of graph paper and find the central point.
3 Line this up with the central point of the top border so that there are the same number of spaces used on either side.
4 Glue the name into position and use this as your pattern.
5 To add the date, time of arrival and weight follow the method described above.
6 Frame the finished embroidery in a toning pastel frame.

Four of the strings on the parachute do not descend at an angle of 45°. When stitching these it is helpful to lay a strand of tacking (basting) thread tautly between the two points to be joined. Use this as a guide for your back stitching and remove the tacking (basting) thread when the strings are completed.

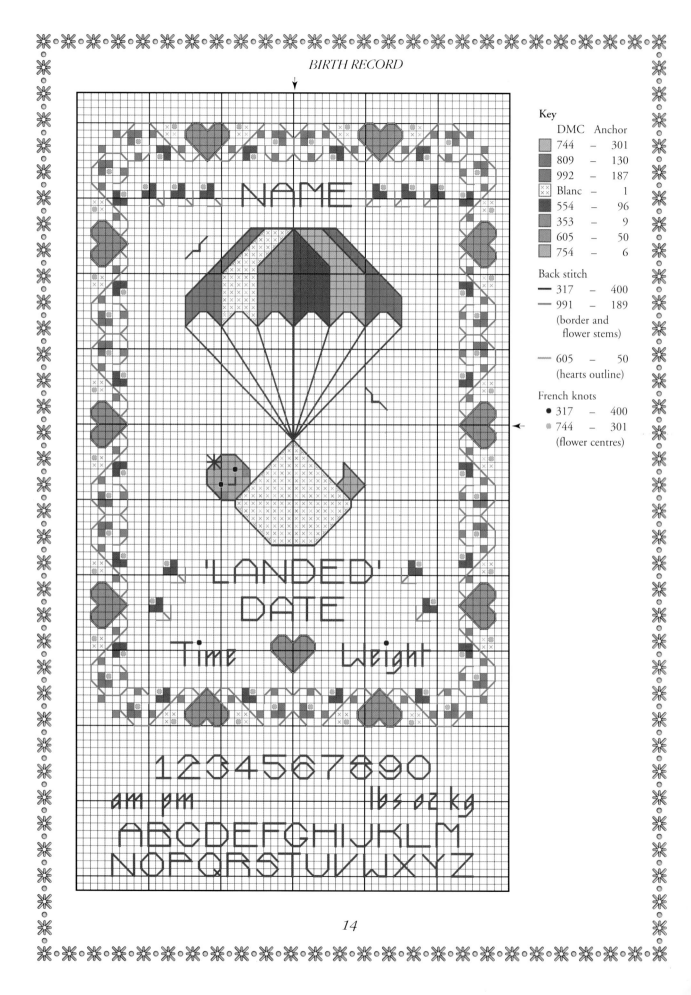

Key

DMC	Anchor
744	– 301
809	– 130
992	– 187
Blanc	– 1
554	– 96
353	– 9
605	– 50
754	– 6

Back stitch

—	317	– 400
—	991	– 189

(border and flower stems)

—	605	– 50

(hearts outline)

French knots

●	317	– 400
●	744	– 301

(flower centres)

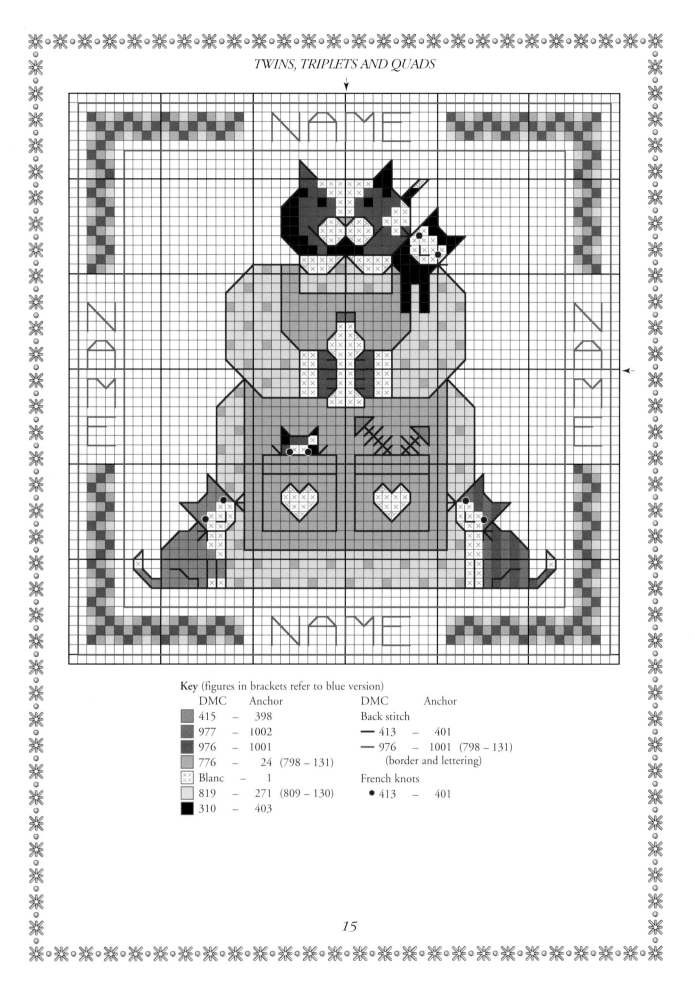

Key (figures in brackets refer to blue version)

	DMC		Anchor	
	415	–	398	
	977	–	1002	
	976	–	1001	
	776	–	24	(798 – 131)
××	Blanc	–	1	
	819	–	271	(809 – 130)
	310	–	403	

DMC   Anchor

Back stitch

— 413 – 401

— 976 – 1001 (798 – 131)
   (border and lettering)

French knots

● 413 – 401

Twins, Triplets and Quads

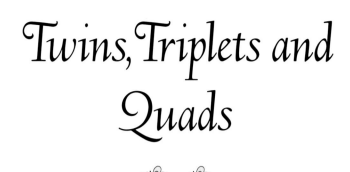

This design was produced shortly after my two kittens, Tipsy and Tom, took up residence. They dominate the household and their constant antics provided the inspiration for this design. The photograph on page 17 shows the design adapted to celebrate the birth of twins and triplets. For quads, stitch all four kittens (chart page 15); for triplets, omit the kitten peeping out of the apron pocket; for twins, stitch only the kittens at the mother cat's feet. Longer names can be used if less of the border pattern is stitched. Use the alphabet and numbers on page 14 to add names and dates.

FINISHED SIZE — picture 4½ x 4½in (11.5 x 11.5cm)
— card 3½ x 3½in (9 x 9cm)

YOU WILL NEED:
8 x 8in (20 x 20cm) Zweigart Linda fabric, colour 264/ivory
Stranded cottons (floss) as in the colour key
Tapestry needle, size 26
For the card version:
Card mount with a window 4 x 4in (10 x 10cm)
Trimmings of your choice

Use 2 strands of stranded cotton (floss) to work all cross stitches. Work back stitches and French knots with 1 strand.

When stitching is complete, either frame the work or mount it into a card using the instructions on page 117. Trim the card with bows, lace or whatever takes your fancy.

(opposite) Twins, Triplets and Quads with Baby's First Mobile

Avoid starting and finishing threads with a knot. Knots form lumps which are particularly evident when work is mounted into a card. Weave loose ends of thread into the back of the stitching and trim the ends off neatly.

Baby's First Mobile

*Stitch a pretty mobile which will bring delight to any nursery. I
made mobiles for both my daughters when they were babies; these
were much enjoyed despite the fact that they were constructed from
wire coat hangers. I will have to wait a few years yet to present this
far more decorative version to my future grandchildren.*

FINISHED SIZE of each heart 3½ x 5in (9 x 13cm)

YOU WILL NEED:

8 pieces 7 x 7in (18 x 18cm) 11 count Aida fabric, colour
   264/cream
Stranded cottons (floss) as in the colour key
Tapestry needle, size 24
Thick white card or mounting board
Tracing paper
Spray Mount adhesive
UHU glue
3¼ yards (3 metres) cream picot-edged ribbon ¼in
   (5mm) wide
8in (20cm) wooden ring
1in (2.5cm) brass curtain ring
Cream paint
6¼ yards (5.75 metres) 1.5mm (¹⁄₁₆in) Offray ribbon,
   colour 815/cream
Assorted beads
8 small bows of ribbon made from the left-over
   trimmings of the 1.5mm (¹⁄₁₆in) ribbon, or from pastel
   coloured ribbon

*Use 3 strands of stranded cotton (floss) to work all
cross stitches. Work back stitches with 1 strand.
Work each heart twice, to make a total of 8 hearts.
   A little patience is needed when making up the
mobile to ensure that the finished article hangs
straight, but the result is well worth the effort.*

1 Paint the wooden ring with cream paint. Put it
aside to dry.
2 Make a tracing of the heart-shaped template on
page 118.
3 Trace 8 heart shapes onto white card and cut
them out.

4 Spray one side of a card heart with Spray Mount
adhesive and position the card heart, adhesive
side down, over the back of one of the embroidered hearts. Lift the embroidery to the light to
check that the card is correctly positioned, adjusting the placement if necessary.
5 Cut away the excess fabric leaving ¾in (2cm)
fabric all round the card. Clip close to the edge of
the embroidery at regular intervals all round.
6 With the back facing you, spread glue close to
the edge of the card, fold the clipped fabric over
and glue down (Fig 3).

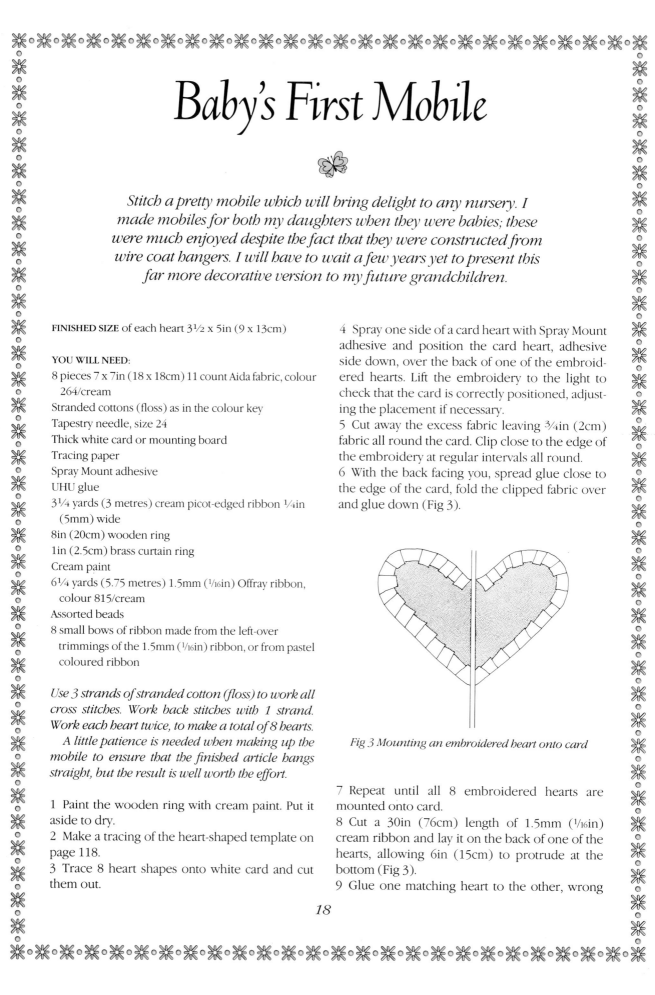

Fig 3 Mounting an embroidered heart onto card

7 Repeat until all 8 embroidered hearts are
mounted onto card.
8 Cut a 30in (76cm) length of 1.5mm (¹⁄₁₆in)
cream ribbon and lay it on the back of one of the
hearts, allowing 6in (15cm) to protrude at the
bottom (Fig 3).
9 Glue one matching heart to the other, wrong

sides together, sandwiching the ribbon between the two. Repeat until you have 4 hearts completed.

10 Glue 2 pieces of picot-edged ribbon to the edge of each heart, one each side of the protruding ribbons, to cover the joins.

11 Trim the ribbons above and below the hearts with assorted beads, using a generous dab of glue to hold the lowest beads in place.

12 Hang the curtain ring from a ceiling hook. Cut two 38in (96cm) lengths and one 24in (61cm) length of 1.5mm (¹/₁₆in) cream ribbon. Fold each length in half forming a loop in the middle. Pass the loops through the curtain ring and pass the ends through the loops to mount the ribbons onto the ring.

13 Tie the painted wooden ring to the 4 long ribbons at regular spacings and distance from the curtain ring (Fig 4). Do not tighten knots until you are satisfied that the spacing is correct and that the wooden ring is hanging straight.

14 Tie the 4 hearts to the wooden ring, again spacing them evenly between the hanging ribbons. Hang each heart at a different level (Fig 4).

15 Trim off the ends of ribbon from which the hearts are suspended and trim the ends of ribbons below the hearts.

16 String beads onto the ends of ribbons coming from the knots on the wooden ring between the hearts, and also onto the two short ribbons hanging from the curtain ring. Use a generous dab of glue to hold all the bottom beads in place. Trim off the ends of the ribbons.

17 Glue a length of picot-edged ribbon around the outside of the wooden ring to hide the knots, and repeat on the inside of the wooden ring.

18 Trim the wooden ring with bows of ribbon at regular intervals.

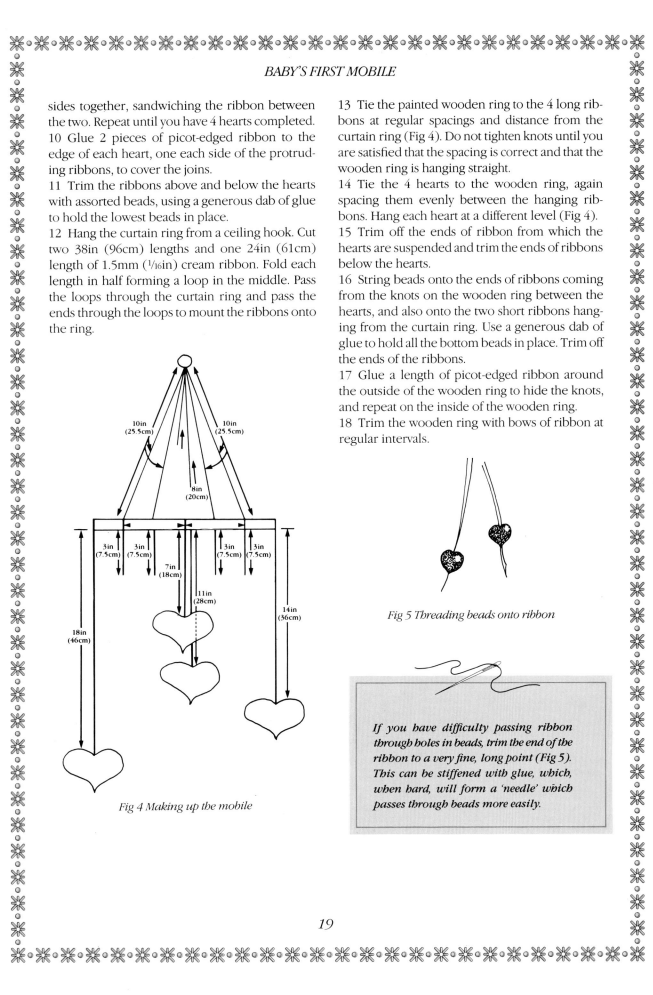

Fig 4 Making up the mobile

Fig 5 Threading beads onto ribbon

If you have difficulty passing ribbon through holes in beads, trim the end of the ribbon to a very fine, long point (Fig 5). This can be stiffened with glue, which, when hard, will form a 'needle' which passes through beads more easily.

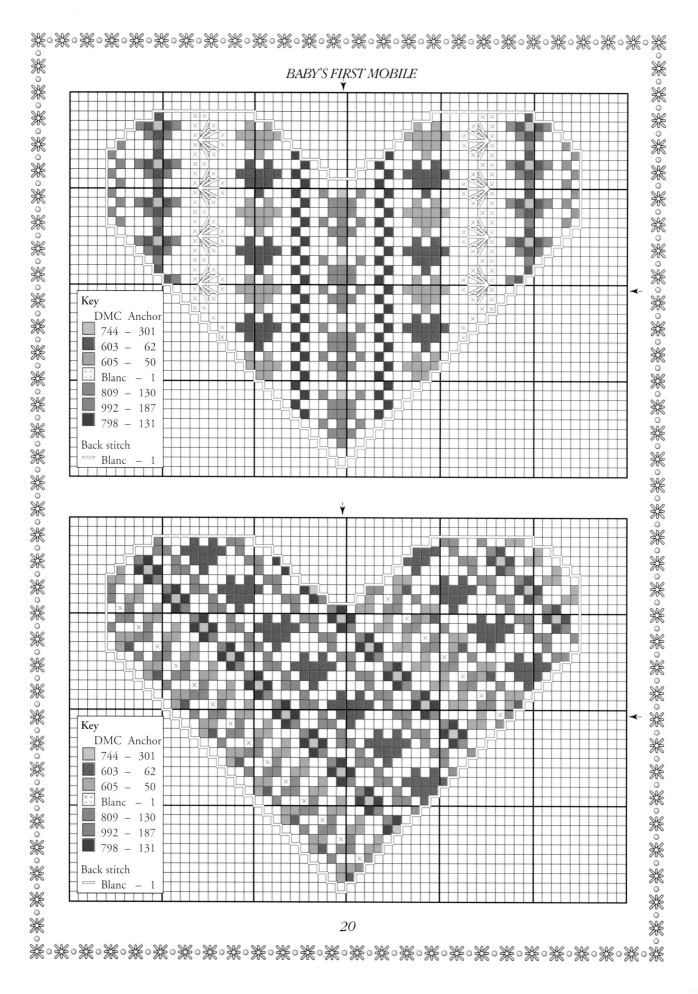

BABY'S FIRST MOBILE

Key
DMC Anchor
744 – 301
603 – 62
605 – 50
Blanc – 1
809 – 130
992 – 187
798 – 131

Back stitch
Blanc – 1

Key
DMC Anchor
744 – 301
603 – 62
605 – 50
Blanc – 1
809 – 130
992 – 187
798 – 131

Back stitch
Blanc – 1

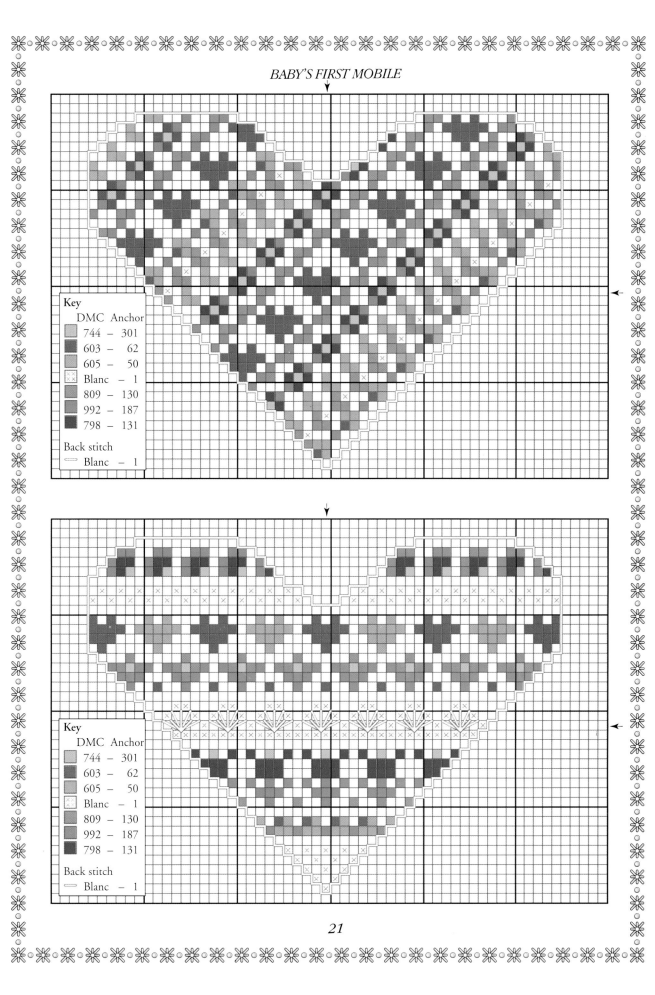

Key

DMC   Anchor
744 – 301
603 – 62
605 – 50
Blanc – 1
809 – 130
992 – 187
798 – 131

Back stitch
Blanc – 1

Key

DMC   Anchor
744 – 301
603 – 62
605 – 50
Blanc – 1
809 – 130
992 – 187
798 – 131

Back stitch
Blanc – 1

Monday's Child

If my rhyme (see pages 26–7) differs from the more traditional version, it is to spare Wednesday's child the sad fate of being full of woe and to update the description of the child that is born on the Sabbath day. Each picture makes an unusual gift to mark the day of the week on which the child was born.

FINISHED SIZE Monday to Saturday 6 x 4½in (15 x 11.5cm) Sabbath 7 x 5½in (18 x 14cm)

YOU WILL NEED:

12 x 10in (30 x 25cm) Zweigart Linda fabric, colour 264/ivory

Stranded cottons (floss) as in the colour key

Tapestry needle, size 26

Beadesign embroidery beads, colours 32/green and 209/gold

Invisible nylon sewing thread

Use 2 strands of stranded cotton (floss) to work all cross stitches. Work back stitches with 1 strand. Work the Algerian eyelets in the border with 2 strands over 2 threads, see Fig 2, page 11.

Using invisible thread, stitch a bead at the points marked with a dot on the chart. Alternate green and gold beads all the way round. The finished embroidery could be mounted as a card, or framed in a small frame.

Key

	DMC	Anchor
	3772	– 1007
	677	– 886
	3752	– 1032
	Blanc	– 1
	993	– 186
	210	– 108
	208	– 111
	3609	– 85

Back stitch

— 413 – 401

— 993 – 186
(leaves on flowers)

Algerian eyelets

✳ 210 – 108

Beadesign embroidery beads

● 209 gold

● 32 green

Key

DMC		Anchor
677	–	886
Blanc	–	1
993	–	186
3752	–	1032
334	–	977
3688	–	66
3689	–	49

Back stitch

413	–	401
993	–	186

(leaves on flowers)

Algerian eyelets

3752 – 1032

Beadesign
embroidery beads
- 209 gold
- 32 green

Key

DMC		Anchor
677	–	886
Blanc	–	1
993	–	186
3752	–	1032
3689	–	49
3688	–	66

Back stitch

413	–	401
993	–	186

(leaves on flowers)

Algerian eyelets

3689 – 49

Beadesign
embroidery beads
- 209 gold
- 32 green

Key

DMC		Anchor
3772	–	1007
677	–	886
Blanc	–	1
3350	–	65
993	–	186
598	–	167
597	–	168

Back stitch
| 413 | – | 401 |
| 993 | – | 186 |

(leaves on flowers)

Algerian eyelets
598 – 167

Beadesign
embroidery beads
209 gold
32 green

Key

DMC		Anchor
677	–	886
Blanc	–	1
993	–	186
341	–	117
340	–	118
598	–	167
3609	–	85

Back stitch
| 413 | – | 401 |
| 993 | – | 186 |

(leaves on flowers)

Algerian eyelets
341 – 117

Beadesign
embroidery beads
209 gold
32 green

Key

DMC		Anchor
414	–	235
415	–	398
3772	–	1007
677	–	886
334	–	977
Blanc	–	1
993	–	186
760	–	1022
3712	–	1023

Back stitch
— 413 – 401
— 993 – 186
(leaves on flowers)

Algerian eyelets
※ 760 – 1022

Beadesign
embroidery beads
● 209 gold
● 32 green

Key

DMC		Anchor
677	–	886
Blanc	–	1
993	–	186
210	–	108
208	–	111

Back stitch
— 413 – 401
— 993 – 186
(leaves on flowers)

Algerian eyelets
※ 210 – 108

Beadesign
embroidery beads
● 209 gold
● 32 green

Christening Shawl

Make your own heirloom with this simple pattern, which repeats to produce a delectable effect. When buying the fabric, ensure that it is cut so that you have 8 x 8 squares on which to embroider (Fig 6), plus half a square all round which will be frayed to make a fringe.

FINISHED SIZE of each square 5 x 5in (12.5 x 12.5cm)

YOU WILL NEED:
51 x 51in (130 x 130cm) Zweigart Anne fabric
DMC Flower threads or stranded cottons (floss) as in the colour key
Tapestry needle, size 24
White sewing thread

Use 2 strands of DMC Flower thread or stranded cotton (floss) to work all cross stitches. Work back stitches with 1 strand.

1 Only half the shawl need be worked. When folded in half triangularly the unworked half is not seen and conveniently covers the back of the stitching. Starting at the bottom point of the shawl, stitch the pattern onto every other square as in Fig 6.
2 Prepare each square which is to be embroidered by tacking (basting) diagonally from corner to corner to find the centre.
3 Stitch the centre of the butterfly's body at the tacked (basted) central point. Remove the tacking (basting) threads at the end of the work.
4 Machine stitch along the edge of the shawl with white sewing thread, using a fine zig-zag stitch.
5 Fray the edge of the shawl up to the line of machine stitching to make a fringe.

CHRISTENING SHAWL

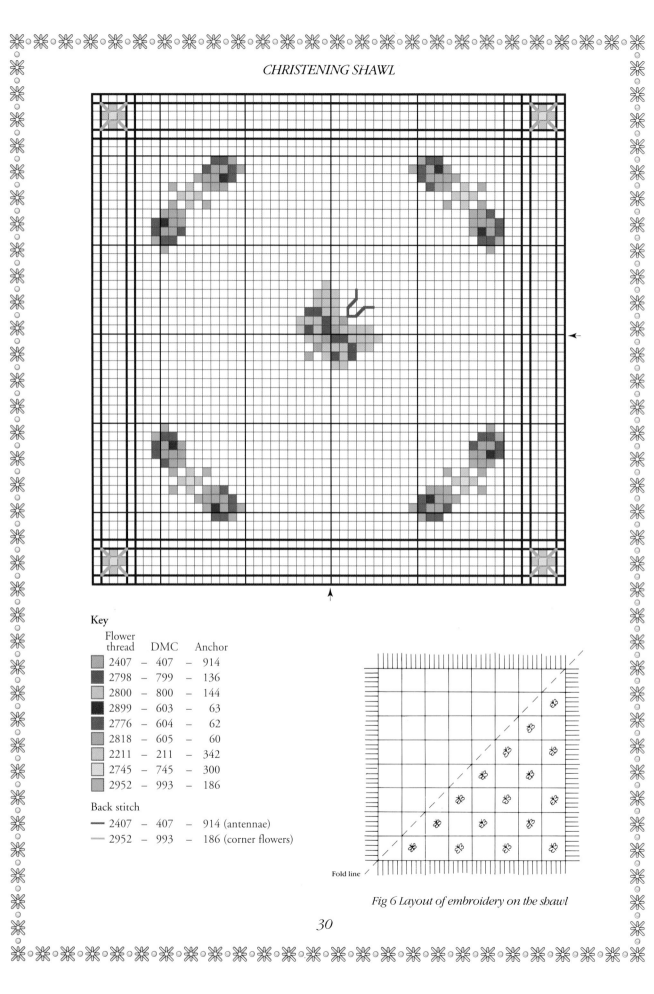

Key

Flower thread	DMC	Anchor	
2407	– 407	–	914
2798	– 799	–	136
2800	– 800	–	144
2899	– 603	–	63
2776	– 604	–	62
2818	– 605	–	60
2211	– 211	–	342
2745	– 745	–	300
2952	– 993	–	186

Back stitch

2407	– 407	–	914 (antennae)
2952	– 993	–	186 (corner flowers)

Fold line

Fig 6 Layout of embroidery on the shawl

Christening Pin Pillow

This confection which welcomes a baby into the fellowship of the church is based on maternity pincushions of the eighteenth and nineteenth centuries which were presented to mothers-to-be. Lettering and numbers are spelled out with pinstuck beads, which also highlight the flowers and butterflies woven into the damask fabric. Under no circumstances allow babies or children to play with the pillow; it is stuck with pins and loose beads which could cause injury. This is definitely a gift to be enjoyed with the eyes and not the fingers.

FINISHED SIZE of pillow 7 x 7in (18 x 18cm)

YOU WILL NEED:
1 square 8 x 8in (20 x 20cm) Zweigart Favourite fabric
Stranded cottons (floss) as in the colour key
Tapestry needle, size 24
8 x 8in (20 x 20cm) white backing fabric
2 pieces 8 x 8in (20 x 20cm) calico
Stuffing
White sewing thread
2 yards (2 metres) broderie anglaise lace 3in (7.5cm) wide
1 yard (1 metre) fine braid or lace
Beadesign beads, colours 80/yellow (flower centres), 89/pink (antennae), 21/blue (lettering)
Fine pins
Trimmings

Use 2 strands of stranded cotton (floss) to work all cross stitches. Work back stitches with 1 strand.

1 To make a cushion pad, place the two pieces of calico right sides together and seam around allowing ½in (1.5cm) seam allowance. Leave an opening in one side. Turn right side out, stuff firmly and slipstitch the opening closed.

2 When the embroidery is complete, place the backing fabric and the embroidered fabric right sides together and seam around allowing ½in (1.5cm) seam allowance. Leave an opening in one side. Turn right side out, insert the cushion pad and slipstitch the opening closed.

3 Using white sewing thread, sew the ends of the broderie anglaise lace together and neaten any raw edges.

4 Gather the lace into a frill, using a small running stitch.

5 Distribute the gathers evenly and stitch the frill around the edge of the pillow.

6 Stitch braid or lace around the pillow, covering the bottom of the broderie anglaise.

7 Trim the corners of the pillow with bows of ribbon, ribbon roses or trimmings of your choice.

8 Work the lettering and date by threading beads onto pins and then pushing the pins firmly into the pillow at the points marked with a dot on the chart. Highlight flower centres and butterflies with more pinstuck beads.

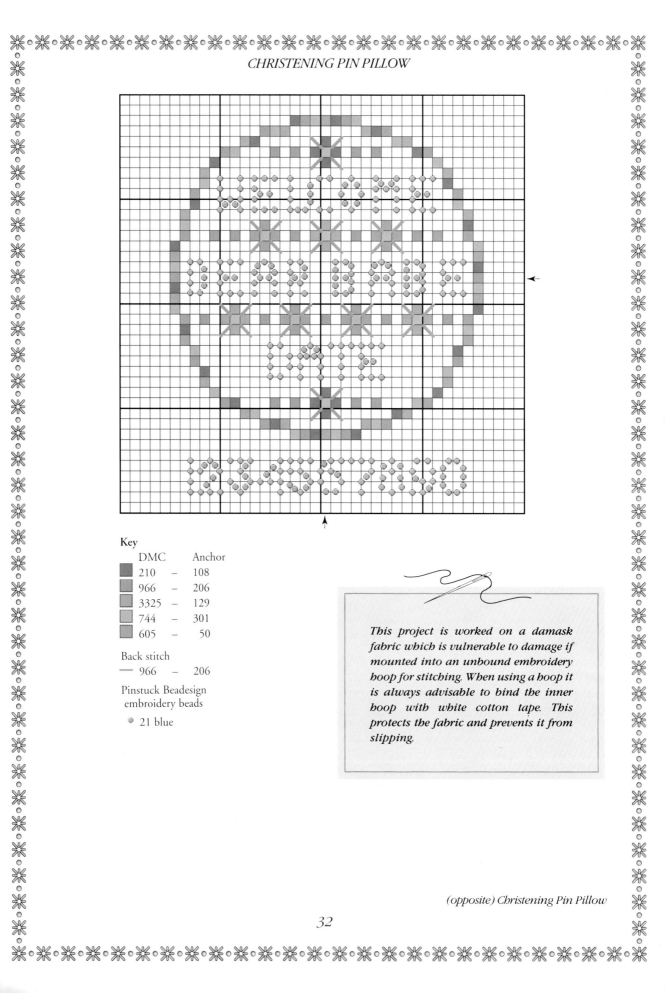

Key

	DMC		Anchor
	210	–	108
	966	–	206
	3325	–	129
	744	–	301
	605	–	50

Back stitch

— 966 – 206

Pinstuck Beadesign
embroidery beads

● 21 blue

This project is worked on a damask fabric which is vulnerable to damage if mounted into an unbound embroidery hoop for stitching. When using a hoop it is always advisable to bind the inner hoop with white cotton tape. This protects the fabric and prevents it from slipping.

(opposite) Christening Pin Pillow

Height Chart

Children enjoy having their height measured and seeing the evidence of their growth. My own children, though now both taller than me, still insist on a regular measuring session, the results of which are marked on the kitchen door frame.
This sunflower makes the exercise fun as children can grow from leaf to leaf. As they gain in height the tape measure can be repositioned and the chart moved up the wall.
If you think that this height chart will be in use for many years, the design can be extended. You could use a longer piece of fabric and stitch extra pairs of leaves to make a taller sunflower. Or, simpler still, add a few more free-flying butterflies at the top.

FINISHED SIZE 8 x 22in (20 x 56cm)

YOU WILL NEED:
12 x 30in (30 x 76cm) 11 count Aida fabric, colour 264/cream
Stranded cottons (floss) as in the colour key
Tapestry needle, size 24
8 x 30in (20 x 76cm) iron-on Vilene
Cream sewing thread
1 pair 8in (20cm) wooden bellpull ends
1 tape measure

Use 3 strands of stranded cotton (floss) to work all cross stitches. Work back stitches and French knots with 1 strand.

1 Find the point on the fabric which is 4in (10cm) up from the bottom and 3in (7.5cm) in from the right-hand side. Mark this temporarily with a pin.
2 Start stitching the bottom right-hand corner of the watering can at this marked point and remove the pin.
3 When the embroidery is complete, iron the Vilene onto the wrong side of the work leaving 2in (5cm) of bare fabric down each side.

4 Turn a 2in (5cm) hem to the wrong side on each side and slipstitch into place.
5 Neaten the top and the bottom and fold each end over a bellpull end.
6 On the wrong side slipstitch the ends of the fabric to hold the bellpull ends in place.
7 Stitch or glue a tape measure to the left-hand side of the chart and hang it on the wall at the correct level.

To ensure good coverage of the fabric when stitching, it is advisable not to allow twists to develop on the thread. At regular intervals let the needle dangle freely from the work. This removes any twists and allows the strands to lie smoothly. You will find this particularly useful when stitching large areas of dark stitches onto light fabric, as with the leaves of this sunflower.

HEIGHT CHART

Key

DMC   Anchor
518   –   168
3761   –   928
743   –   302
433   –   371
742   –   303
699   –   923
701   –   227
321   –   9046
898   –   360
907   –   255
310   –   403
Blanc –   1
415   –   398

Back stitch
—   310   –   403

French knots
●   310   –   403

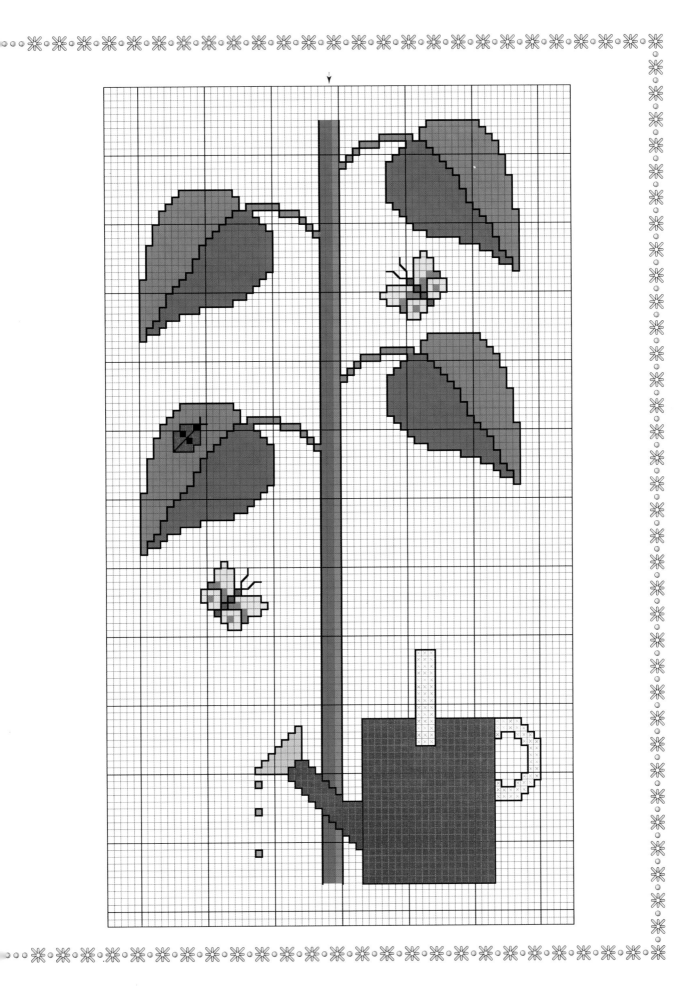

Alphabet Game

Help a child to learn the alphabet painlessly with this colourful
and decorative game (overleaf). If a lesson can be fun it is
willingly learned. Here the object of the game is to match the
pictures to the letters correctly.

FINISHED SIZE 18½ x 15½in (47 x 39.5cm)

YOU WILL NEED:
For the board: 28 x 25in (71 x 64cm) 14 count Aida
   fabric, colour 264/cream
7½ yards (6.75 metres) Offray 1.5mm (¹/₁₆in) ribbon,
   colour 250/red
Stranded cottons (floss) as in the colour key
Tapestry needle, size 26
40in (1 metre) white Velcro fastening tape, ⅝in (1.5cm)
   wide
Cream sewing thread
Brass paper fasteners
For the pictures: 42 x 24in (107 x 61cm) 14 count Aida
   fabric, colour 264/cream
1 sheet strong white card (mounting board) or 2 sheets
   14-mesh plastic canvas 8 x 11in (20 x 28cm)
14 x 8in (36 x 20cm) white felt

*Use 2 strands of stranded cotton (floss) to work all
cross stitches. Work couching and back stitches
with 1 strand. The lines framing each letter on the
board are worked by couching down lengths of
ribbon, but cross stitches can be substituted.*

1 From the ribbon, cut five 22in (56cm) lengths
for the horizontal lines, and eight 19in (48cm)
lengths for the vertical lines.
2 Couch the ribbon to the surface of the fabric
(Fig 1, page 11) to form the frames for each letter.
Pierce a small hole at the end of each line and
thread the ends of the ribbons to the back of the
work. Hold the ends neatly in place with a slipstitch.
3 Stitch the letters of the alphabet in the top left-
hand corners of the frames. The corner of each
frame is marked on the alphabet chart.

4 When the embroidery of the board is complete,
cut twenty-six 1½in (3.5cm) lengths of Velcro,
and using cream sewing thread, stitch a piece of
Velcro in each frame in the position marked on the
chart.
5 To stitch the pictures, cut the fabric into twenty-
six 6in (15cm) squares and work one design on
each.
6 Cut twenty-six 2in (5cm) squares of stiff white
card.
7 Lay a square of card over the back of one of the
pictures and trim the excess fabric away to ½in
(1.5cm) all round.
8 With cream sewing thread, lace the fabric across
the back of the card, from side to side and from top
to bottom (Fig 7a).

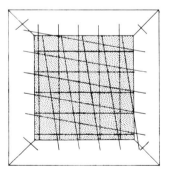

Fig 7a Lacing work onto card

9 Cut a 1¾ x 1¾in (4.5 x 4.5cm) square of white
felt and stitch this to the back of the picture to
hide the lacing.
10 Stitch a piece of Velcro to the back of the
picture (Fig 7b). Repeat steps 7 to 10 until all the
pictures are completed.

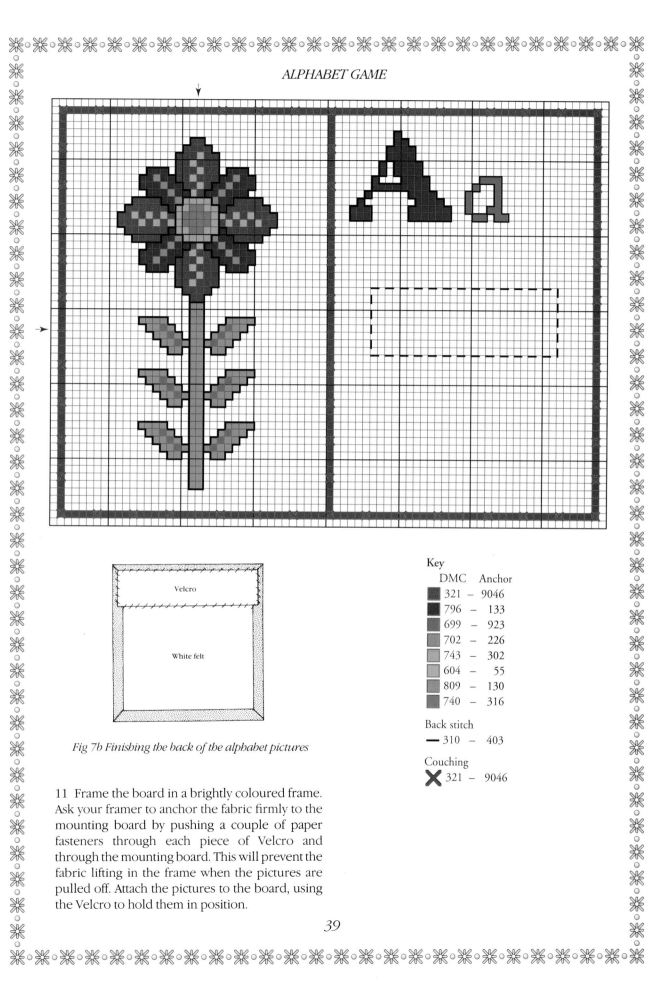

Fig 7b Finishing the back of the alphabet pictures

Key

DMC		Anchor
321	–	9046
796	–	133
699	–	923
702	–	226
743	–	302
604	–	55
809	–	130
740	–	316

Back stitch
— 310 – 403

Couching
✘ 321 – 9046

11 Frame the board in a brightly coloured frame. Ask your framer to anchor the fabric firmly to the mounting board by pushing a couple of paper fasteners through each piece of Velcro and through the mounting board. This will prevent the fabric lifting in the frame when the pictures are pulled off. Attach the pictures to the board, using the Velcro to hold them in position.

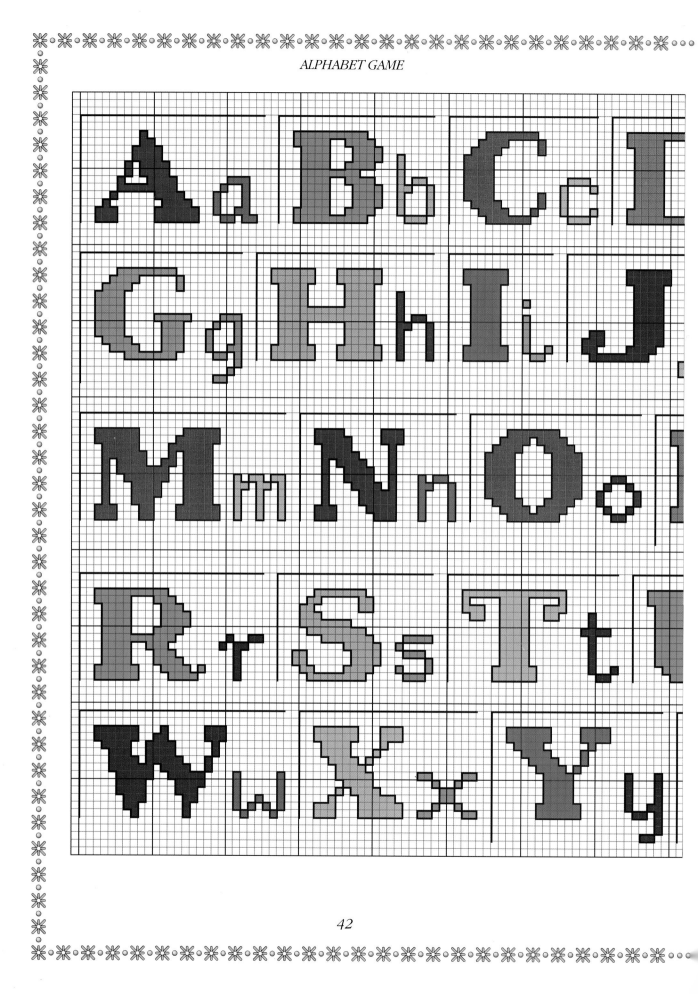

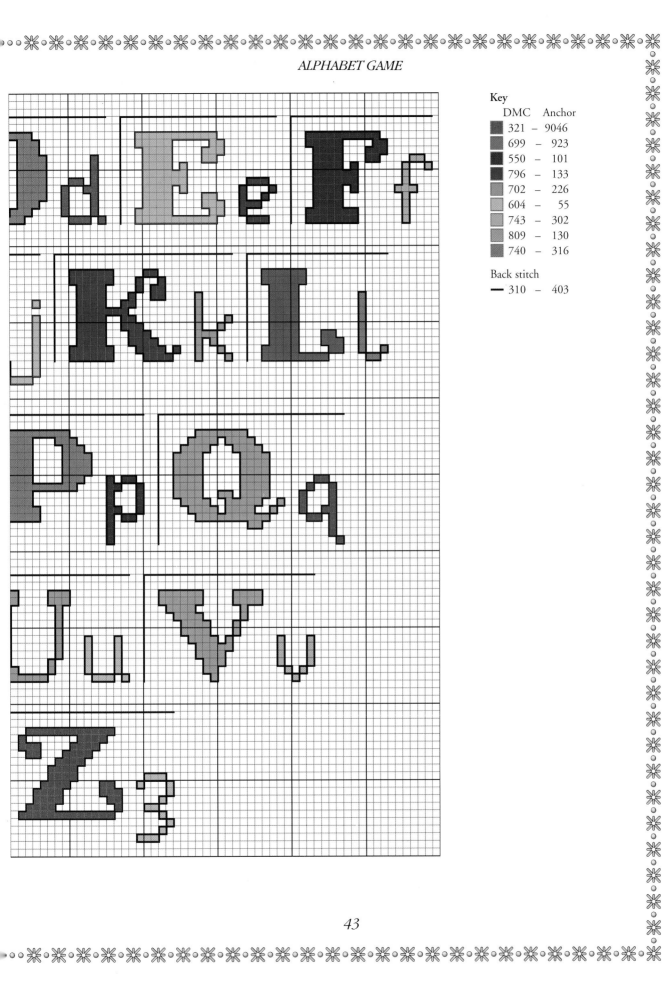

Key

	DMC	Anchor
	321	–	9046
	699	–	923
	550	–	101
	796	–	133
	702	–	226
	604	–	55
	743	–	302
	809	–	130
	740	–	316

Back stitch
— 310 – 403

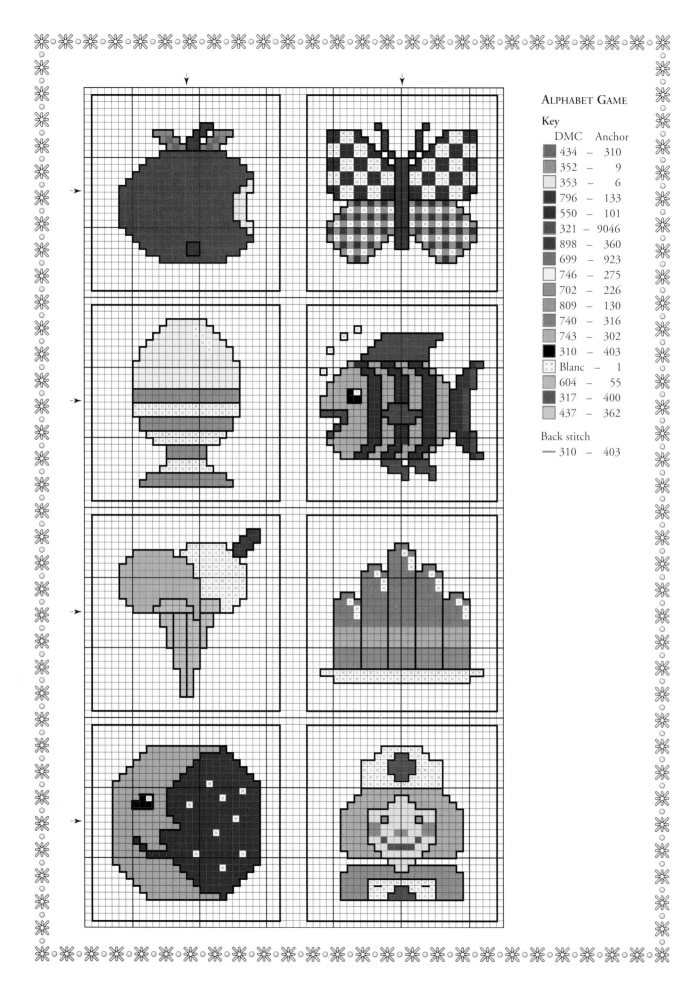

ALPHABET GAME

Key

	DMC		Anchor
	434	–	310
	352	–	9
	353	–	6
	796	–	133
	550	–	101
	321	–	9046
	898	–	360
	699	–	923
	746	–	275
	702	–	226
	809	–	130
	740	–	316
	743	–	302
	310	–	403
☒	Blanc	–	1
	604	–	55
	317	–	400
	437	–	362

Back stitch

| | 310 | – | 403 |

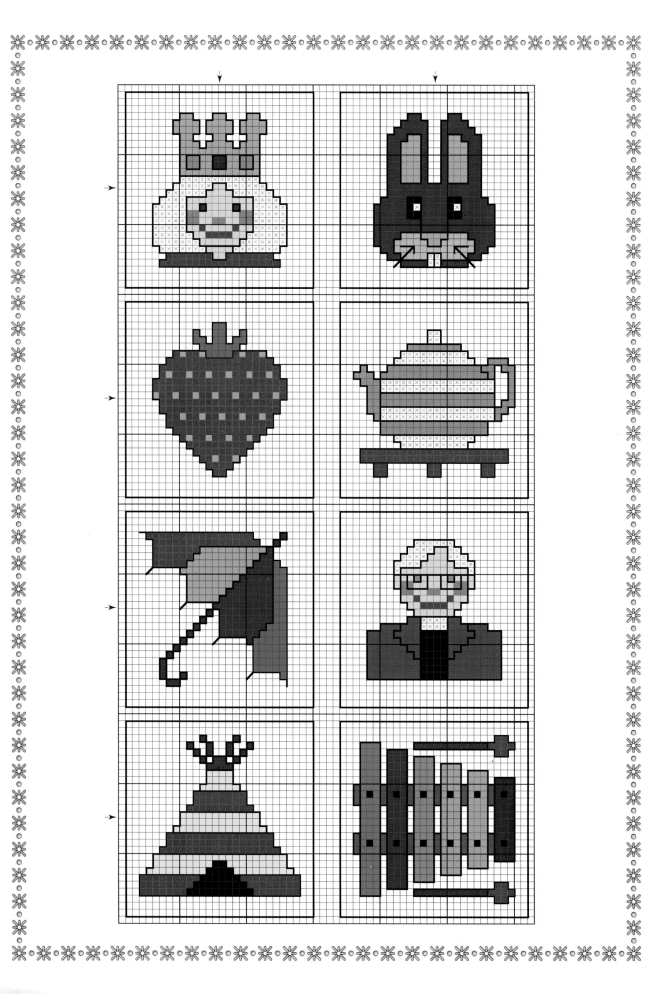

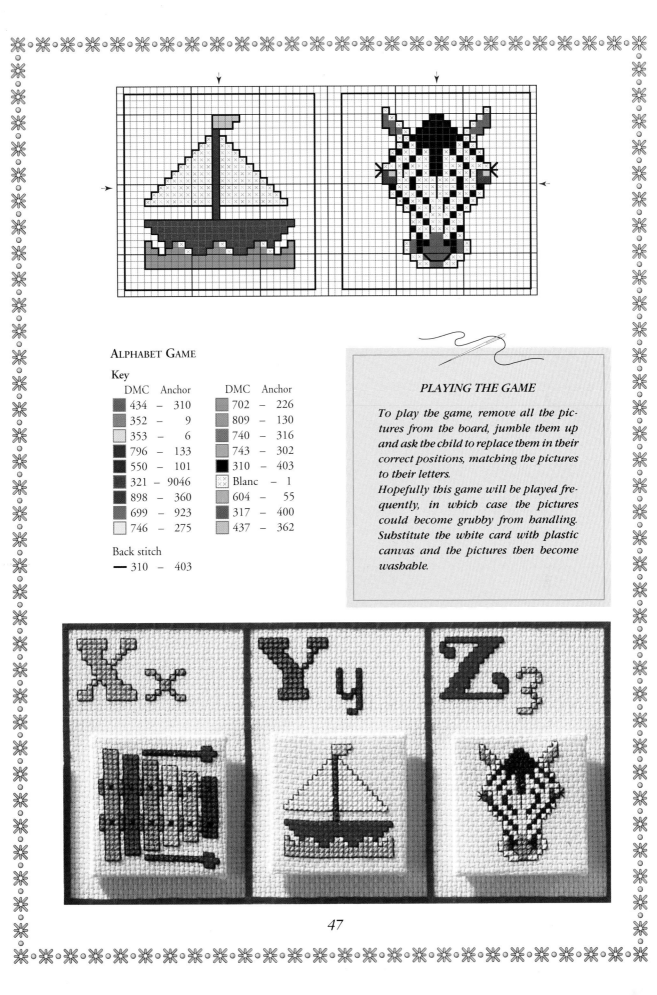

ALPHABET GAME

Key

DMC	Anchor	DMC	Anchor
434 – 310		702 – 226	
352 – 9		809 – 130	
353 – 6		740 – 316	
796 – 133		743 – 302	
550 – 101		310 – 403	
321 – 9046		Blanc – 1	
898 – 360		604 – 55	
699 – 923		317 – 400	
746 – 275		437 – 362	

Back stitch
— 310 – 403

PLAYING THE GAME

To play the game, remove all the pictures from the board, jumble them up and ask the child to replace them in their correct positions, matching the pictures to their letters.

Hopefully this game will be played frequently, in which case the pictures could become grubby from handling. Substitute the white card with plastic canvas and the pictures then become washable.

Learn to Count

Counting is easy with this simple design which features novelty buttons. These were collected at craft fairs, but similar buttons are widely available at good haberdashers and collecting them is all part of the fun.

FINISHED SIZE 11½ x 9in (29 x 23cm)

YOU WILL NEED:

18 x 15in (46 x 38cm) 11 count Aida fabric, colour 264/cream
Stranded cottons (floss) as in the colour key
Tapestry needle, size 24
55 Novelty buttons, assorted colours
Cream sewing thread
Frame

Use 3 strands to work all cross stitches.

Plan ahead when buying the buttons to get a good range of colours. Choose buttons which contrast well with the colour of the lettering. For example, avoid having blue buttons next to blue lettering.

When all the embroidery is complete, stitch on the buttons at the points marked X on the chart, using cream sewing thread. Frame the finished design in a brightly coloured frame.

Try not to give in to the temptation to stitch on the buttons as you complete each line; your embroidery thread will continually get caught up in them.

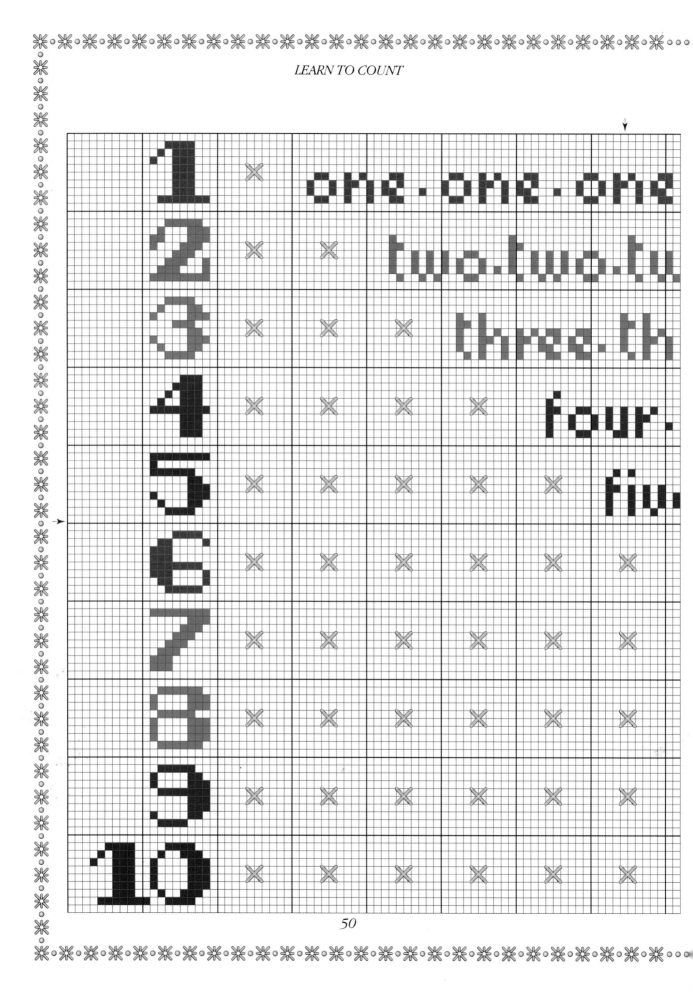

1 one.one.one
2 two.two.tw
3 three.th
4 four.
5 fiv
6
7
8
9
10

Key

DMC		Anchor
740	–	316
699	–	923
824	–	164
321	–	9046
550	–	101

Weather Calendar

'The north wind doth blow, and we shall have snow', or maybe rain, fog, sun or thunder. Every morning a child can change the date on this calendar and put a pointer to the season and weather conditions. It might be fun to play weather forecaster at bedtime and try to predict what is in store for the next day.

FINISHED SIZE 7¾ x 7¾in (19.5 x 19.5cm)

YOU WILL NEED:
For the board: 15 x 15in (38 x 38cm) Zweigart Linda fabric, colour 264/ivory
For the dates, numbers and arrows: 1 sheet 14-mesh plastic canvas 8 x 11in (20 x 28cm)
Stranded cottons (floss) as in the colour key
Tapestry needles, sizes 26 and 24
16 white 20mm (¾in) Velcro Spot Ons
1 yard (1 metre) white Velcro fastening tape, ⅝in (1.5cm) wide
White sewing thread
Brass paper fasteners

For the board, use 2 strands of stranded cotton (floss) to work all cross stitches. Work back stitches and French knots with 1 strand.

For the dates and arrows, use 3 strands to work all cross stitches. Work edging stitch with 6 strands.

1 When the embroidery of the board is complete, stitch Velcro Spot Ons (furry sides only) around the outside of the weather symbols, placing the edge of the spots at the points marked – on the chart. Stitch lengths of Velcro tape (furry side only) in the central space in the positions indicated by dotted lines on the chart.
2 Frame the board in a brightly coloured frame. Ask your framer to anchor the fabric firmly to the mounting board by pushing a paper fastener through each piece of Velcro and through the mounting board. This will prevent the fabric lifting in the frame when the dates and arrows are pulled off.

3 Dates and arrows, which will be subjected to frequent handling, are worked on plastic canvas to make them durable and easily washable. Work each date and cut it out leaving one square of plastic canvas all round to hold the edging stitch. Use cross stitch to completely cover the plastic canvas and edge each piece with edging stitch (Fig 8). Work the numbers 1 and 2 twice each, and work 3 arrows.

Fig 8 Edging stitch

4 Stitch a Velcro Spot On (looped side only) to the back of each arrow.
5 Stitch lengths of Velcro tape (looped side only) to the back of the dates, trimming the width of the tape to fit the dates and cover the back of the work.
6 Put the dates in a small bag or box for safe keeping, and place this near the calendar.

EDGING STITCH
Always bring the needle from the wrong side of the canvas and pull the thread through to the front, working the holes in the following sequence:
1, 3, 2, 4, 3, 5, 4, 6, 5, 7, 6, 8 etc.

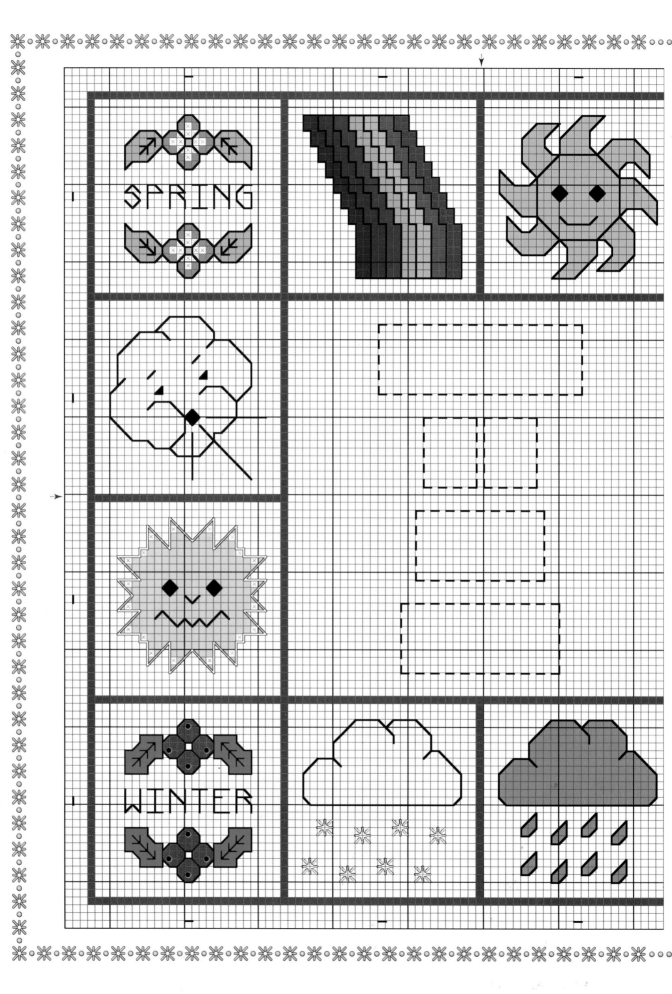

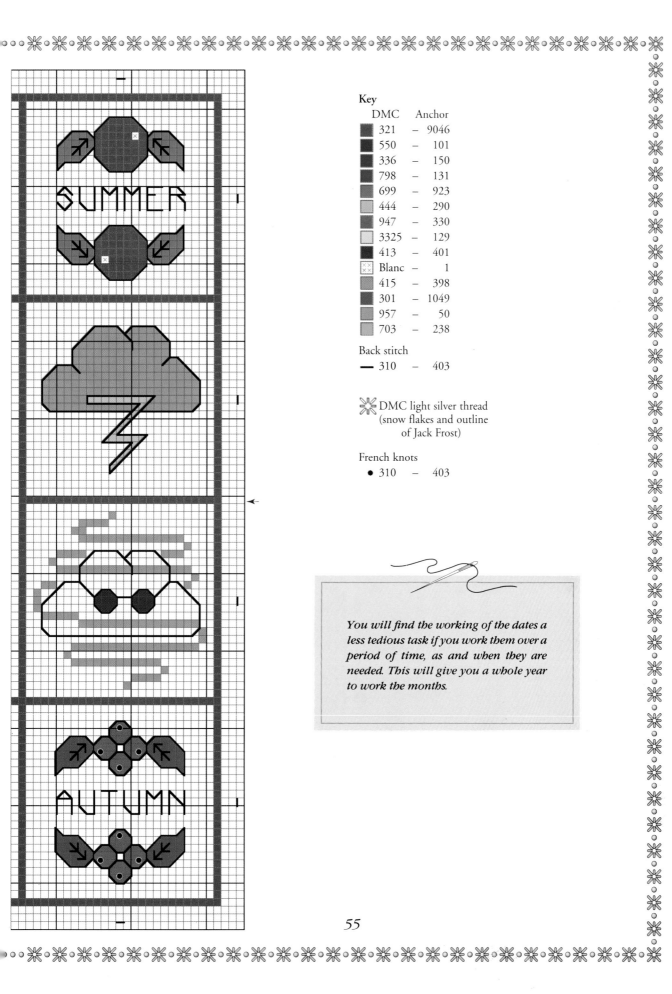

Key

DMC		Anchor
321	–	9046
550	–	101
336	–	150
798	–	131
699	–	923
444	–	290
947	–	330
3325	–	129
413	–	401
Blanc	–	1
415	–	398
301	–	1049
957	–	50
703	–	238

Back stitch

— 310 – 403

☀ DMC light silver thread
(snow flakes and outline
of Jack Frost)

French knots

● 310 – 403

*You will find the working of the dates a
less tedious task if you work them over a
period of time, as and when they are
needed. This will give you a whole year
to work the months.*

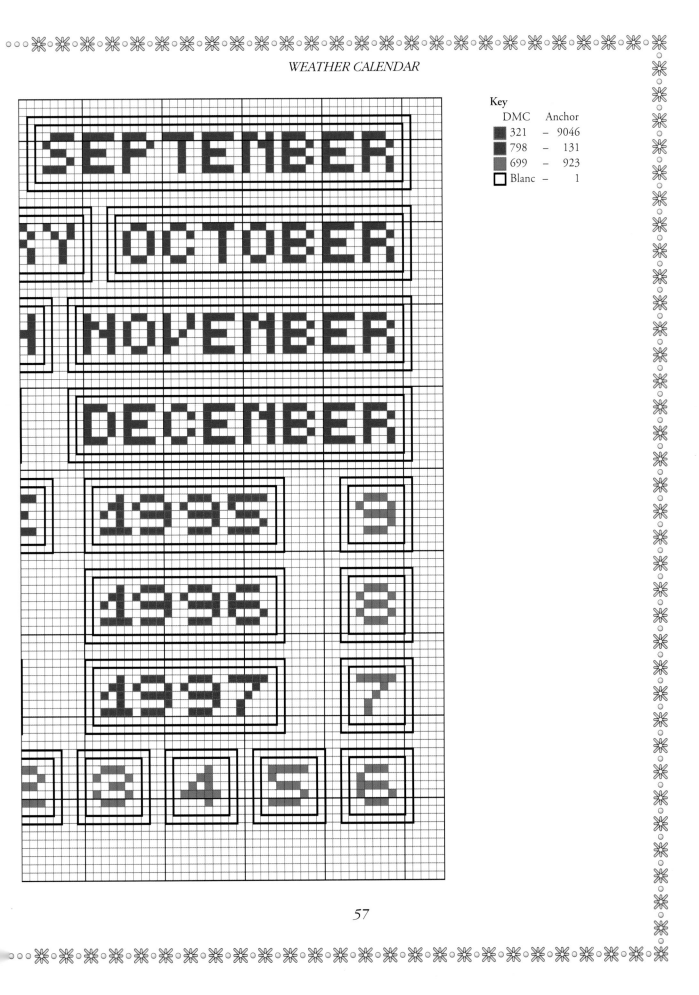

Key

DMC	Anchor
321 –	9046
798 –	131
699 –	923
Blanc –	1

Advent Calendar

Anticipating Christmas is one of the most exciting times for children. Make this Advent calendar and you will never have to buy another. It can be brought out year after year and will become as much a part of your family's Christmas as the fairy that sits on top of the tree.

FINISHED SIZE of each triangle 5½ x 6½in (14 x 16.5cm)

YOU WILL NEED:

7 x 43in wide (18 x 110cm) 11 count Aida fabric, colour 1/white

14 x 43in wide (36 x 110cm) 11 count Aida fabric, colour 670/green

Stranded cottons (floss) as in the colour key

Tapestry needle, size 24

Tracing paper

Scraps of red, white or green backing fabric to back the triangles

Stuffing

25 ¾in (2cm) brass curtain rings

1 1in (2.5cm) brass curtain ring

21in (53cm) dowel ¼in (5mm) thick, optional

20 jingle bells

20 small bows of red ribbon

12 x 4in (30.5 x 10cm) brown fabric (trunk)

13 x 8in (33 x 20cm) red fabric (pot)

13 x 8in (33 x 20cm) red backing fabric (pot)

Scraps of tartan ribbon to trim the pot

1 large tartan ribbon bow

Sewing thread

Use 3 strands to work all cross stitches. Work back stitches with 2 strands.

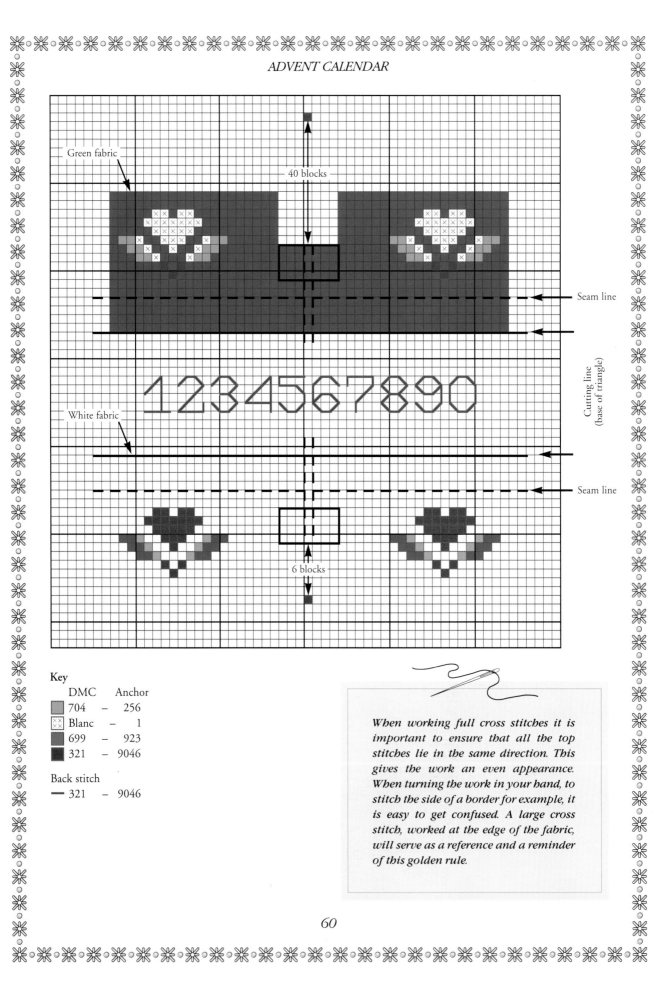

Green fabric

40 blocks

Seam line

Cutting line
(base of triangle)

1234567890

White fabric

Seam line

6 blocks

Key

DMC		Anchor
704	–	256
Blanc	–	1
699	–	923
321	–	9046

Back stitch
— 321 – 9046

When working full cross stitches it is important to ensure that all the top stitches lie in the same direction. This gives the work an even appearance. When turning the work in your hand, to stitch the side of a border for example, it is easy to get confused. A large cross stitch, worked at the edge of the fabric, will serve as a reference and a reminder of this golden rule.

1 Make a tracing of the triangular pattern on page 118 and use this as a pattern to cut 10 triangles of white Aida fabric and 15 triangles of green Aida fabric (Fig 9). Line up the pattern so that the base of each triangle is cut between blocks along the straight grain of the fabric.

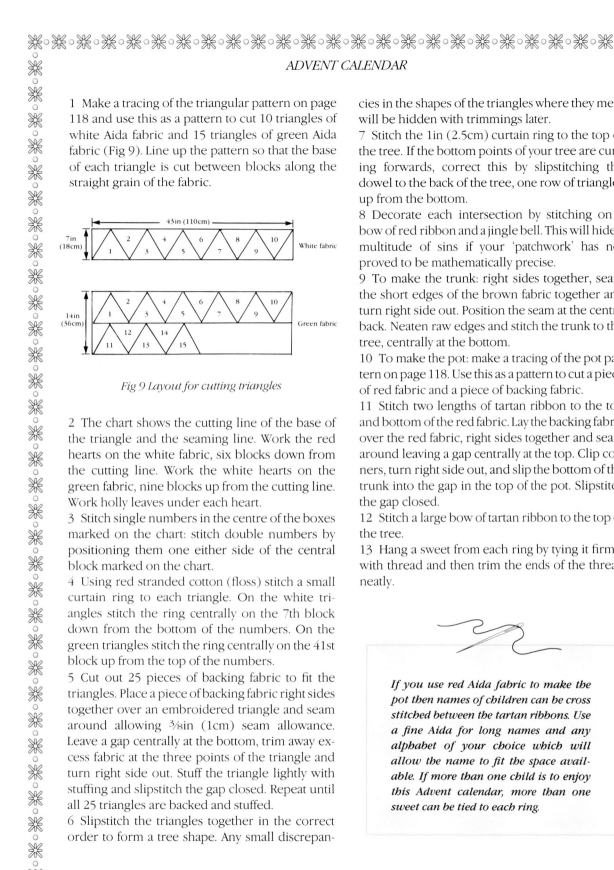

Fig 9 Layout for cutting triangles

2 The chart shows the cutting line of the base of the triangle and the seaming line. Work the red hearts on the white fabric, six blocks down from the cutting line. Work the white hearts on the green fabric, nine blocks up from the cutting line. Work holly leaves under each heart.

3 Stitch single numbers in the centre of the boxes marked on the chart: stitch double numbers by positioning them one either side of the central block marked on the chart.

4 Using red stranded cotton (floss) stitch a small curtain ring to each triangle. On the white triangles stitch the ring centrally on the 7th block down from the bottom of the numbers. On the green triangles stitch the ring centrally on the 41st block up from the top of the numbers.

5 Cut out 25 pieces of backing fabric to fit the triangles. Place a piece of backing fabric right sides together over an embroidered triangle and seam around allowing ⅜in (1cm) seam allowance. Leave a gap centrally at the bottom, trim away excess fabric at the three points of the triangle and turn right side out. Stuff the triangle lightly with stuffing and slipstitch the gap closed. Repeat until all 25 triangles are backed and stuffed.

6 Slipstitch the triangles together in the correct order to form a tree shape. Any small discrepan-

cies in the shapes of the triangles where they meet will be hidden with trimmings later.

7 Stitch the 1in (2.5cm) curtain ring to the top of the tree. If the bottom points of your tree are curling forwards, correct this by slipstitching the dowel to the back of the tree, one row of triangles up from the bottom.

8 Decorate each intersection by stitching on a bow of red ribbon and a jingle bell. This will hide a multitude of sins if your 'patchwork' has not proved to be mathematically precise.

9 To make the trunk: right sides together, seam the short edges of the brown fabric together and turn right side out. Position the seam at the centre back. Neaten raw edges and stitch the trunk to the tree, centrally at the bottom.

10 To make the pot: make a tracing of the pot pattern on page 118. Use this as a pattern to cut a piece of red fabric and a piece of backing fabric.

11 Stitch two lengths of tartan ribbon to the top and bottom of the red fabric. Lay the backing fabric over the red fabric, right sides together and seam around leaving a gap centrally at the top. Clip corners, turn right side out, and slip the bottom of the trunk into the gap in the top of the pot. Slipstitch the gap closed.

12 Stitch a large bow of tartan ribbon to the top of the tree.

13 Hang a sweet from each ring by tying it firmly with thread and then trim the ends of the thread neatly.

If you use red Aida fabric to make the pot then names of children can be cross stitched between the tartan ribbons. Use a fine Aida for long names and any alphabet of your choice which will allow the name to fit the space available. If more than one child is to enjoy this Advent calendar, more than one sweet can be tied to each ring.

Christmas Stocking

On Christmas Eve it is customary to provide a glass of Christmas cheer with a mince pie for Santa and a brussel sprout for Rudolph Invariably Santa has had one sherry too many by the time he reaches my house, but this dazzling stocking will help him to remember the reason for his visit.

FINISHED SIZE 12 x 10¾in (30.5 x 27cm)

YOU WILL NEED:
16 x 16in (41 x 41cm) 11 count Aida fabric, colour 954/red
Stranded cottons (floss) as in the colour key
Tapestry needle, size 24
16 x 16in (41 x 41cm) red backing fabric
2 pieces of lining fabric 16 x 16in (41 x 41cm)
18 x 14in (46 x 35.5cm) white fur fabric
Short lengths of fancy braids
1½ yards (1.5 metres) Christmas piping cord
White sewing thread
Red sewing thread

Use 3 strands of stranded cotton (floss) to work all cross stitches. Work back stitches and French knots with 1 strand.

1 Using white sewing thread, back stitch the outline of the stocking centrally onto the Aida fabric.
2 In the top band stitch a short name, or initials, using the holly alphabet on page 65.
3 When all the embroidery is completed, stitch lengths of braid between the bands of embroidery, extending ½in (1.5cm) beyond the white back stitched outline.
4 Place the backing fabric, right sides together, over the Aida fabric. Using red sewing thread, stitch the two together following the white outline and catching the ends of the braids in the seam. Leave the top of the stocking open.
5 Trim the seam to ½in (1.5cm), clip curves and turn right side out.
6 Unpick all traces of the white back stitch outline.
7 Stitch the two pieces of lining fabric right sides together, using the shape of the stocking as a stitching guide and leaving the top open. Trim the seams to ½in (1.5cm), clip curves and insert into the stocking, wrong sides together, to form a lining.
8 To make the cuff: using white sewing thread, stitch the short sides of the white fur fabric, right sides together, to form a tube (Fig 10, overleaf). Allow ½in (1.5cm) seam allowance. Turn ½in (1.5cm) fabric to the inside, top and bottom, and hem in place (Fig 11). Turn right side out.
9 Fold the cuff in half along the fold line (Fig 11), and slipstitch the cuff to the top of the stocking ½in (1.5cm) down on the outside, and on the inside covering the raw edges of both the stocking and the lining. Place the seam on the cuff on the right-hand side of the stocking.
10 Stitch piping cord along the seam of the stocking, forming a loop hanger at the top on the right. Tie a knot in the remaining piping cord and fray the cord below the knot.

Fancy braids can be expensive and difficult to find. You can add extra glitter to an ordinary braid by sewing sequins and beads along the length of it.

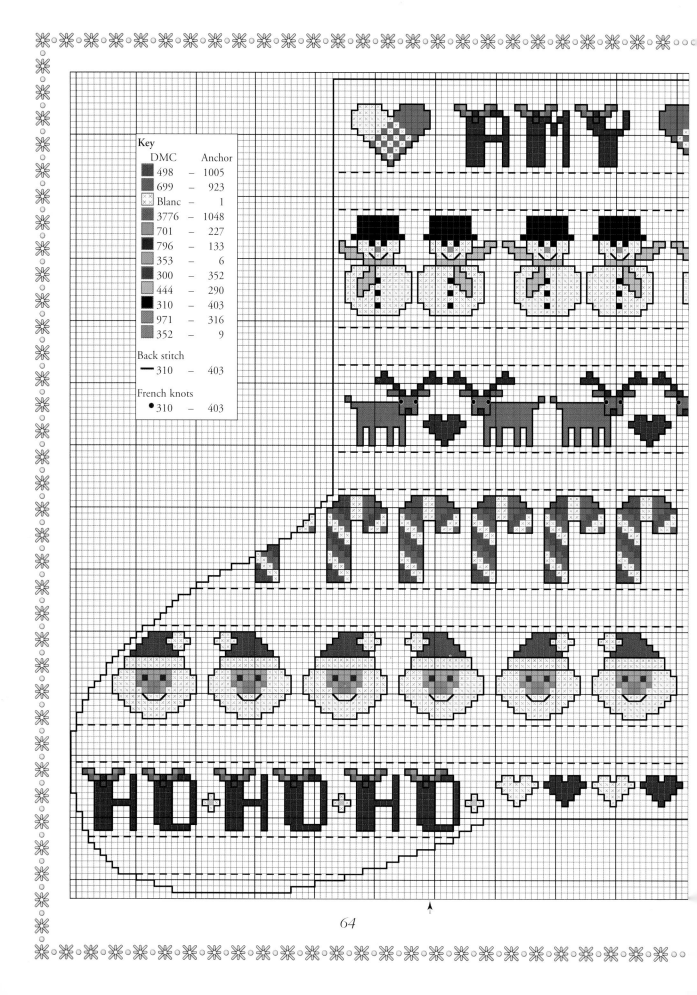

Key

DMC		Anchor
498	–	1005
699	–	923
Blanc	–	1
3776	–	1048
701	–	227
796	–	133
353	–	6
300	–	352
444	–	290
310	–	403
971	–	316
352	–	9

Back stitch
— 310 – 403

French knots
● 310 – 403

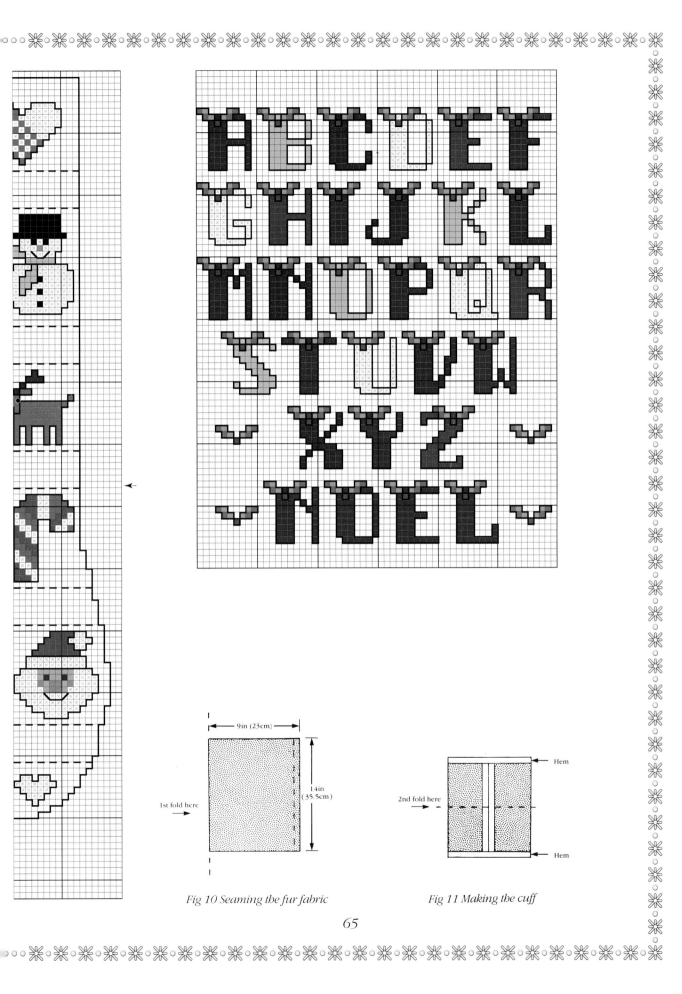

Fig 10 Seaming the fur fabric

Fig 11 Making the cuff

Tooth Fairy Pillow

Take pity on the poor Tooth Fairy who has to hunt in the dark under pillows to find discarded teeth. Pop the tooth into the pocket and place the pillow on the bedside table. You never know, she might be so grateful that she leaves a few extra pennies.

FINISHED SIZE of pillow 4 x 6in (10 x 15cm)

YOU WILL NEED:
Zweigart Linda fabric, colour 264/ivory
   Cut 1 piece 5 x 5in (13 x 13cm) for the quilt (Pattern A)
   Cut 1 piece 7 x 5in (18 x 13cm) for the bed (Pattern B)
   Cut 1 piece 7 x 5in (18 x 13cm) for backing fabric
Stranded cottons (floss) as in the colour key
Tapestry needle, size 26
20in (51cm) cotton lace, 1in (2.5cm) wide
Cream sewing thread
Fibrefill stuffing

Use 2 strands of stranded cotton (floss) to work all cross stitches. Work back stitches and French knots with 1 strand.

1 Stitch Pattern A onto the 5 x 5in (13 x 13cm) piece of fabric. Embroider the bottom left-hand corner of the chart in the bottom left-hand corner of the fabric, allowing ½in (1.5cm) for seams.

2 Stitch Pattern B onto one of the 7 x 5in (18 x 13cm) pieces of fabric. Embroider the top left-hand corner of the chart in the top left-hand corner of the fabric, allowing ½in (1.5cm) for seams.

3 When all the embroidery is complete, turn under the fabric at the top of the quilt. Slipstitch it into place on the wrong side, using cream sewing thread, so that ½in (1.5cm) of sheet is left showing.

4 Tack (baste) the quilt to the bed so that the edge of the sheet comes just below the teddy bear's arms and so that the right sides of both pieces of fabric are face up.

5 Place the backing fabric, right sides together, over the bed and quilt. Seam all the way round, as close as possible to the embroidery, leaving a gap centrally at the bottom of the bed. Clip corners, turn right side out and remove all tacking (basting) thread.

6 Stuff the pillow firmly and slipstitch the gap closed.

7 Neaten the raw edges of the lace. Make a row of small running stitches along the straight edge of the lace. Gather the lace so that it fits around the top outer edge of the bed between the points marked X on the chart. Slipstitch the lace onto the bed, adjusting all gathers so that they are evenly distributed along the seam.

Stranded cottons (floss) never go to waste in my household: left-overs are kept and used for small projects such as this patchwork quilt. Each square could be worked in a different colour to use up scraps of thread.

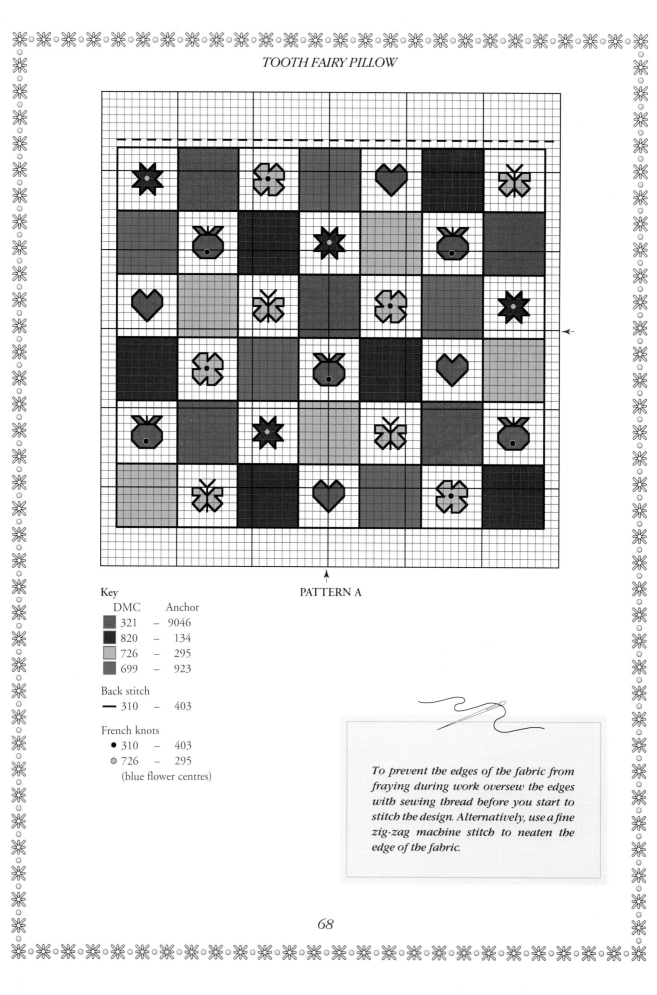

PATTERN A

Key

DMC		Anchor
321	–	9046
820	–	134
726	–	295
699	–	923

Back stitch

— 310 – 403

French knots

● 310 – 403
○ 726 – 295
　(blue flower centres)

To prevent the edges of the fabric from fraying during work oversew the edges with sewing thread before you start to stitch the design. Alternatively, use a fine zig-zag machine stitch to neaten the edge of the fabric.

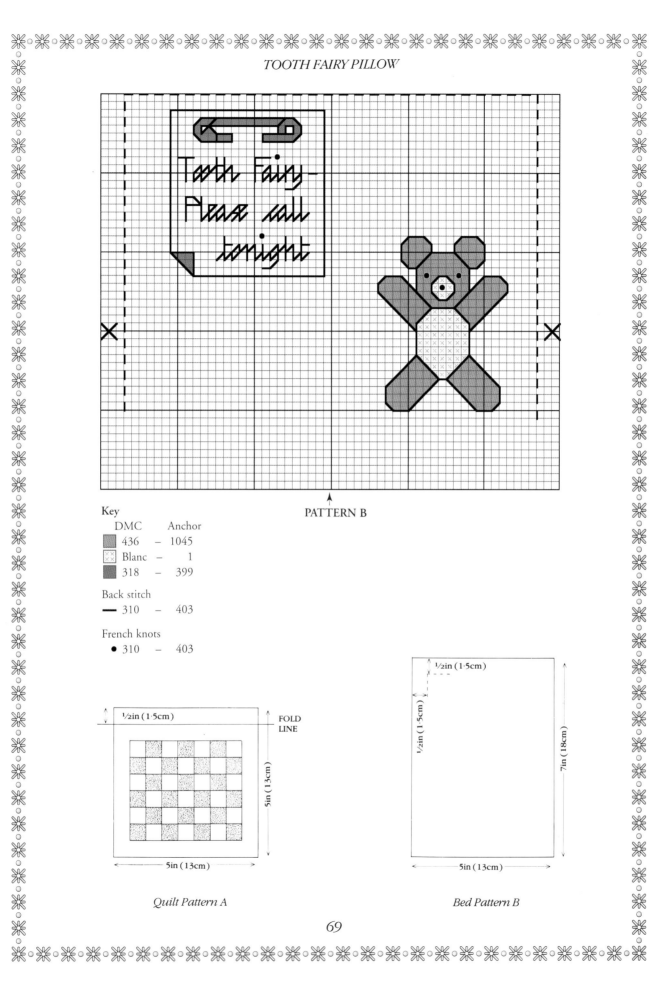

PATTERN B

Key

DMC		Anchor
436	–	1045
Blanc	–	1
318	–	399

Back stitch
— 310 – 403

French knots
● 310 – 403

Quilt Pattern A

Bed Pattern B

Travel Tackle Goody Bag

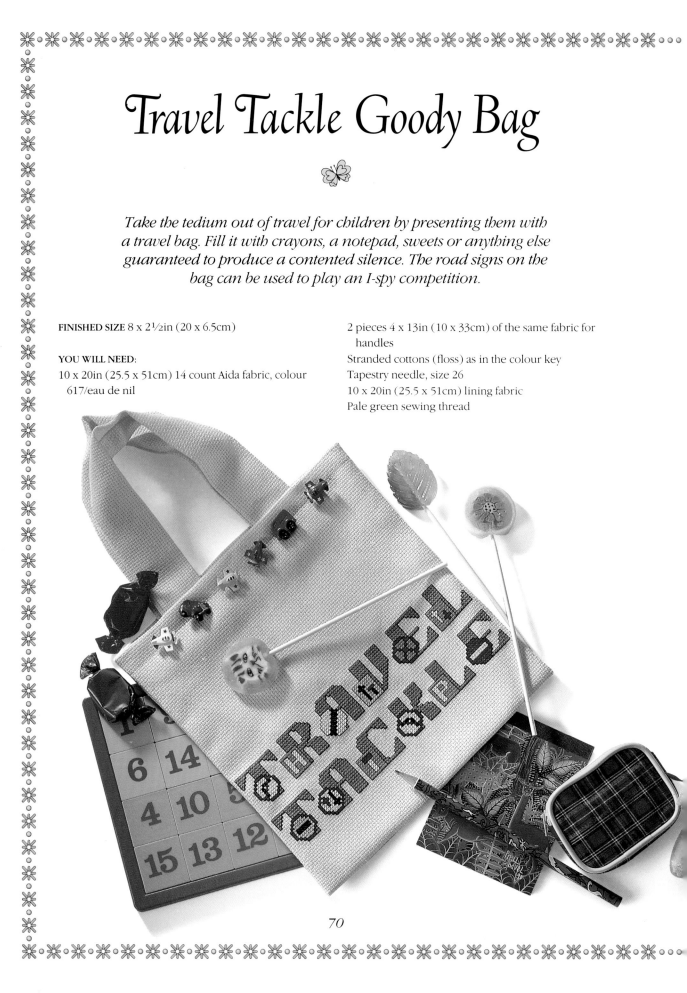

Take the tedium out of travel for children by presenting them with a travel bag. Fill it with crayons, a notepad, sweets or anything else guaranteed to produce a contented silence. The road signs on the bag can be used to play an I-spy competition.

FINISHED SIZE 8 x 2½in (20 x 6.5cm)

YOU WILL NEED:
10 x 20in (25.5 x 51cm) 14 count Aida fabric, colour 617/eau de nil

2 pieces 4 x 13in (10 x 33cm) of the same fabric for handles
Stranded cottons (floss) as in the colour key
Tapestry needle, size 26
10 x 20in (25.5 x 51cm) lining fabric
Pale green sewing thread

Use 2 strands of stranded cotton (floss) to work all cross stitches. Work back stitches with 1 strand.

1 Fold the Aida fabric in half and mark the central point with tacking (basting) thread. Stitch the design centrally 1½in (4cm) up from the fold (Fig 12).

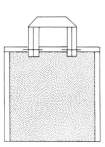

Fig 13 Making the bag

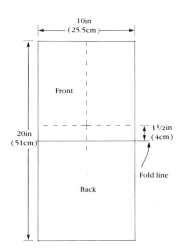

Fig 12 Preparing the bag fabric

2 Fold the fabric in half, right sides together, and seam the two side edges allowing ½in (1.5cm) for seams.

3 Turn a ½in (1.5cm) hem to the inside of the bag and tack (baste) in place.

4 Right sides together, stitch together the long edges of the fabric for the handles, allowing ½in (1.5cm) seam allowance. Turn right side out and press the handles so that the seam is lying centrally at the back of each handle. Stitch one handle to the front of the bag, and one to the back, ¼in (5mm) from the top of the bag (Fig 13). Turn the bag right side out.

5 Repeat step 2 with the lining fabric.

6 Turn a ½in (1.5cm) hem on wrong side of the lining; place the lining into the bag, wrong sides together, and slipstitch in place along the top of the bag. Remove the tacking (basting) threads.

7 Fill the bag with assorted essentials and goodies.

Turning bag handles right side out can be an unnecessarily fiddly performance. Take a piece of waste ribbon or thin tape which is slightly longer than the handle. When folding the fabric place the ribbon inside the tube and secure it with a few stitches at one end, leaving an inch or two of ribbon protruding at the other end. Seam the handle, taking care not to catch the ribbon in the seam. Pull the protruding ribbon to help turn the handle right side out, trim off the ribbon and use it when making the second handle.

School Stuff Goody Bag

A useful and distinctive bag for pencils, erasers, dinner money, conkers, pieces of string, marbles, toffee papers and other such vital possessions.

FINISHED SIZE 7½ x 2½in (19 x 6.5cm)

YOU WILL NEED:

10 x 20in (25.5 x 51cm) 14 count Aida fabric, colour 589/navy

2 pieces 4 x 13in (10 x 33cm) of the same fabric for handles

Stranded cottons (floss) as in the colour key

Tapestry needle, size 26

10 x 20in (25.5 x 51cm) lining fabric

Dark blue sewing thread

Use 2 strands of stranded cotton (floss) to work all cross stitches. Work back stitches with 1 strand.

To work and make up the bag, follow the instructions on page 71.

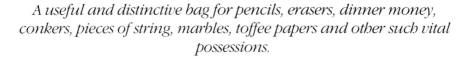

Those of you, unlike me, who do not blench at the idea of putting in a zip could make this design up as a pencil case.

TRAVEL TACKLE
Key

	DMC		Anchor
	726	–	295
	321	–	9046
	Blanc	–	1
	996	–	433
	943	–	188
	310	–	404

Back stitch

— 310 – 403

SCHOOL STUFF
Key

	DMC		Anchor
	973	–	297
	321	–	9046
	Blanc	–	1
	699	–	923
	701	–	227
	208	–	111
	995	–	410
	602	–	57
	310	–	403

Back stitch

— 310 – 403

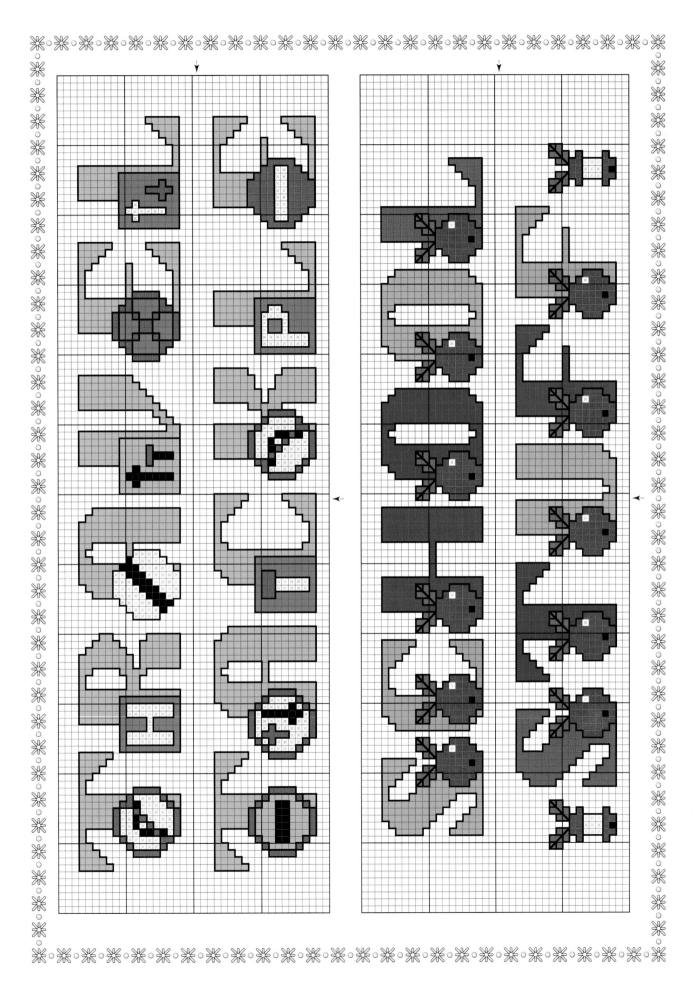

Happy Hols Goody Bag

This is just what is needed to carry essentials like sunglasses, sun cream, a stick of rock and small toys to the beach (see pages 74–5).

FINISHED SIZE 5³⁄4 x 2¹⁄2in (14.5 x 6.5cm)

YOU WILL NEED:

10 x 20in (25.5 x 51cm) 14 count Aida fabric, colour 2/lemon

2 pieces 4 x 13in (10 x 33cm) of the same fabric for handles

Stranded cottons (floss) as in the colour key

Tapestry needle, size 26

10 x 20in (25.5 x 51cm) lining fabric

Pale yellow sewing thread

Use 2 strands of stranded cotton (floss) to work all cross stitches. Work back stitches with 1 strand.

To work and make up the bag, follow the instructions on page 71.

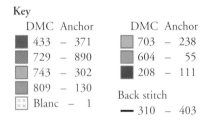

To protect the bag from the ravages of leaking sun cream and damp, sandy shells, it might be a good idea to line this bag with waterproof lining fabric which can be wiped clean.

Key

DMC	Anchor		DMC	Anchor
433	– 371		703	– 238
729	– 890		604	– 55
743	– 302		208	– 111
809	– 130			
Blanc	– 1			

Back stitch

— 310 – 403

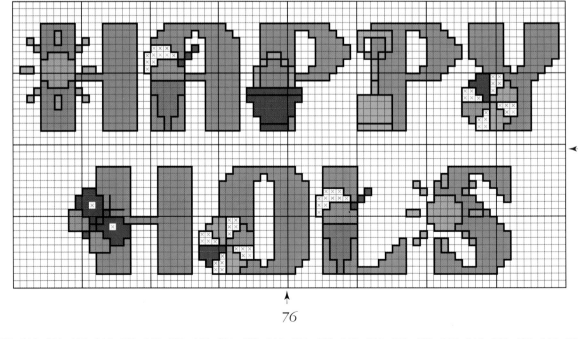

Get Well Goody Bag

If a child is going into hospital, present him or her with this bag (pages 74–5) filled with toiletries and toys to wish them a speedy recovery.

FINISHED SIZE 5 x 2½in (13 x 6.5cm)

YOU WILL NEED:
10 x 20in (25.5 x 51cm) 14 count Aida fabric, colour
  503/sky
2 pieces 4 x 13in (10 x 33cm) of the same fabric for
  handles
Stranded cottons (floss) as in the colour key
Tapestry needle, size 26
10 x 20in (25.5 x 51cm) lining fabric
Pale blue sewing thread

*Use 2 strands of stranded cotton (floss) to work all
cross stitches. Work back stitches with 1 strand.*

To work and make up the bag, follow the instructions on page 71.

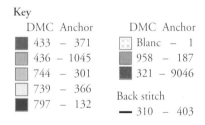

*Finish off each area of a design neatly,
before going on to the next. Work the end
of the thread into the back of existing
stitches and trim close to the work using
sharp, fine-pointed embroidery scissors.*

Key

DMC	Anchor		DMC	Anchor
433	– 371		Blanc	– 1
436	– 1045		958	– 187
744	– 301		321	– 9046
739	– 366			
797	– 132			

Back stitch
— 310 – 403

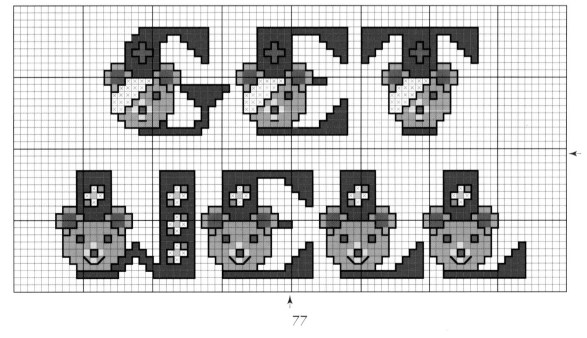

Kitty Bag

This design was modelled by my kittens, Tipsy on the right and Tom on the left. Fill the bag with a grooming comb, catnip mice and other essentials for kitten care. Present the bag to a young owner of a kitten to remind them of their responsibilities.

FINISHED SIZE 6¼ x 2¼in (16 x 6cm)

YOU WILL NEED:

10 x 20in (25.5 x 51cm) 14 count Aida fabric, colour 95/black

2 pieces 4 x 13in (10 x 33cm) of the same fabric for handles

Stranded cottons (floss) as in the colour key

Tapestry needle, size 26

10 x 20in (25.5 x 51cm) lining fabric

Black sewing thread

3½in (9cm) cream parcel twine

Use 2 strands of stranded cotton (floss) to work all cross stitches. Work back stitches with 1 strand.

To work and make up the bag, follow the instructions on page 71.

Unravel the parcel twine and thread lengths of it through the kittens' noses to make whiskers.

Always stitch in a good light. If you find that working on black fabric causes you eye strain, work this design on a light coloured fabric.

Key

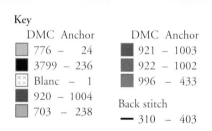

DMC	Anchor		DMC	Anchor
776	– 24		921	– 1003
3799	– 236		922	– 1002
Blanc	– 1		996	– 433
920	– 1004			
703	– 238			

Back stitch
— 310 – 403

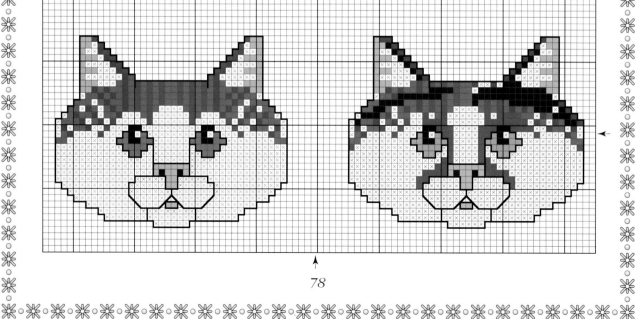

Doggy Bag

This bag is not for left-over restaurant meals, but is designed to hold grooming combs, flea powder, dog biscuits, toys and other doggy requisites. Children adore their puppies and this will add even more pleasure to the arrival of Fido.

FINISHED SIZE 6¼ x 2¼in (16 x 6cm)

YOU WILL NEED:

10 x 20in (25.5 x 51cm) 14 count Aida fabric, colour 264/cream

2 pieces 4 x 13in (10 x 33cm) of the same fabric for handles

Stranded cottons (floss) as in the colour key

Tapestry needle, size 26

10 x 20in (25.5 x 51cm) lining fabric

Cream sewing thread

Use 2 strands of stranded cotton (floss) to work all cross stitches. Work back stitches with 1 strand.

To work and make up the bag, follow the instructions on page 71.

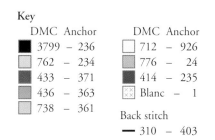

If you make a mistake and have to unpick your work, use sharp fine-pointed embroidery scissors to cut the stitches. Tweezers are useful to remove the offending threads.

Key

DMC	Anchor		DMC	Anchor
3799	236		712	926
762	234		776	24
433	371		414	235
436	363		Blanc	1
738	361			

Back stitch
— 310 – 403

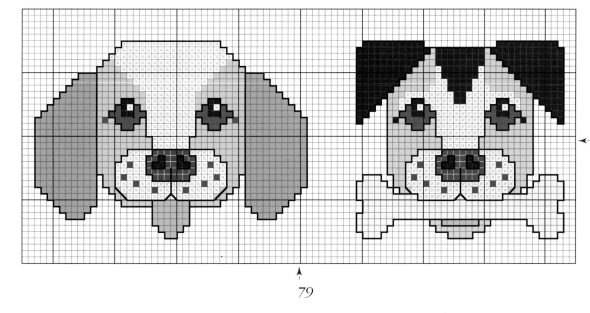

Circus Treat

Stitch a lasting and colourful reminder of a trip to the circus. The design is worked on sawdust-coloured fabric and is mounted into the hoop in which it was worked. When this is bound in red and white thread it then resembles the circus ring.

FINISHED SIZE 7 x 7in (18 x 18cm)

YOU WILL NEED:

12 x 12in (30 x 30cm) Zweigart Linda fabric, colour
  307/beige
12 x 12in (30 x 30cm) white backing fabric
8in (20cm) embroidery hoop
Stranded cottons (floss) as in the colour key
Tapestry needle, size 26
4 brightly coloured feathers
Assorted sequins
Small beads
Beading needle
Beige sewing thread
1 skein DMC Coton Retors Mat, colour blanc/white
1 skein DMC Coton Retors Mat, colour 2304/red
UHU glue
1 yard (1 metre) narrow braid

Use 2 strands of stranded cotton (floss) to work all cross stitches. Work back stitches and French knots with 1 strand.

Before starting to stitch a project, press any stubborn creases out of your fabric. Protect your fabric with a thin, cotton cloth and use a steam iron. This would be unthinkable after the embroidery is completed, as the stitches would be completely flattened.

1 When the embroidery is complete, cut small pieces from the feathers. Push a piece of feather through a sequin and sew on the feathered sequins in the positions marked X on the chart.

2 Using a beading needle and beige sewing thread, sew on small sequins and beads under the clown's umbrella to resemble a shower coming out of the umbrella as he opens it.

3 Bind the embroidery hoop to resemble the circus ring: hold a tape measure around the outside edge of the outer hoop and with a pencil mark off 1in (2.5cm) segments.

4 Spread one segment at a time with a thin film of glue and wrap the DMC Coton Retors Mat tightly around the hoop ensuring that the wood is covered. Bind alternate segments in red and white. Make sure that all the ends of thread are on the inside of the hoop and are stuck down firmly so that they do not become dislodged when the hoop is pressed down over the embroidery.

5 Tack (baste) the backing fabric to the wrong side of the embroidery to form a lining which hides the back of the work.

6 Position the lined embroidery face-up, centrally over the inner hoop. Place the outer hoop over the embroidery and press down into place.

7 Tighten the screw adjuster until the embroidery is evenly stretched in the hoop, easing it into position carefully. Ensure that the screw adjuster is positioned centrally at the top of the design. If it is not, your embroidery will hang at a drunken angle for evermore.

8 Trim away the excess fabric on the wrong side and glue down the raw edges onto the back of the inner hoop. Glue a length of narrow braid over the raw edges to give a neat finish.

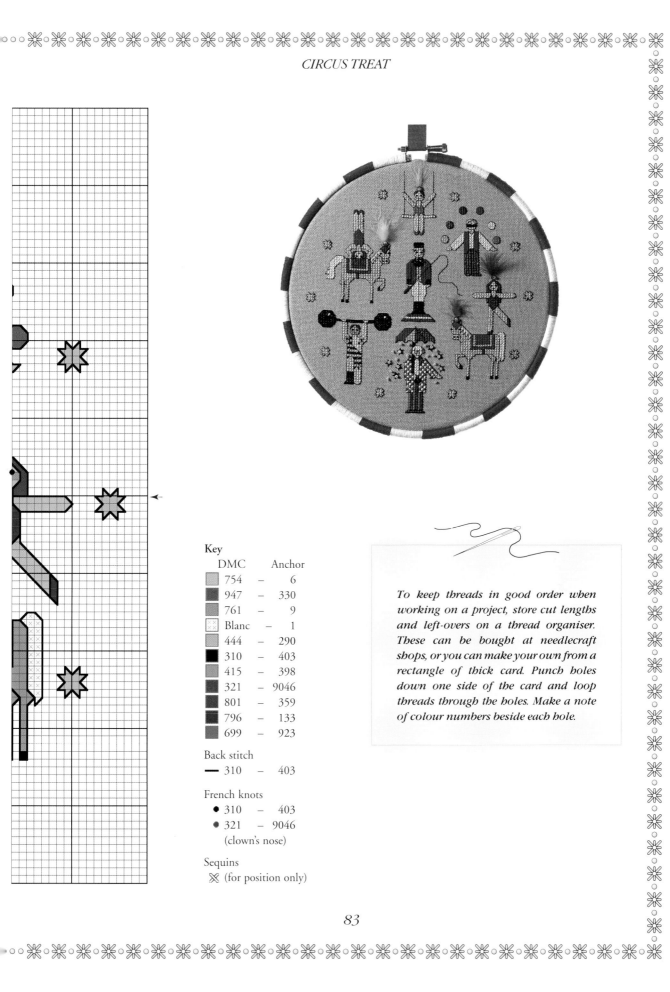

Key

DMC		Anchor
754	–	6
947	–	330
761	–	9
Blanc	–	1
444	–	290
310	–	403
415	–	398
321	–	9046
801	–	359
796	–	133
699	–	923

Back stitch

— 310 – 403

French knots

- 310 – 403
- 321 – 9046
  (clown's nose)

Sequins

※ (for position only)

To keep threads in good order when working on a project, store cut lengths and left-overs on a thread organiser. These can be bought at needlecraft shops, or you can make your own from a rectangle of thick card. Punch holes down one side of the card and loop threads through the holes. Make a note of colour numbers beside each hole.

The Ten Commandments

In 1729 a child named Sarah Cocke stitched a version of Dr Isaac Watts's rhyme in a variety of stitches, following the precept that 'what is learned in verse is longer retained in memory and sooner recollected'. Such was the magnitude of her stitching task that I imagine she never forgot her lesson. As a small child I remember being sent off to Sunday school every week. There I learned the ten commandments by rote, unfortunately without the assistance of this verse.

FINISHED SIZE 14 x 8in (35.5 x 20cm)

YOU WILL NEED:
20 x 14in (51 x 36cm) Zweigart Linda fabric, colour 264/ivory
Stranded cottons (floss) as in the colour key
Tapestry needle, size 26
Oxford frame 16 x 10in (40.5 x 25.5cm), optional

Use 2 strands of stranded cotton (floss) to work all cross stitches. Work back stitches and French knots with 1 strand.

When the embroidery is complete, frame the work in the Oxford frame, or any frame of your choice.

> *Do not be tempted to carry the thread from one word to another across the back of bare fabric, as a ghostly trail will show through.*

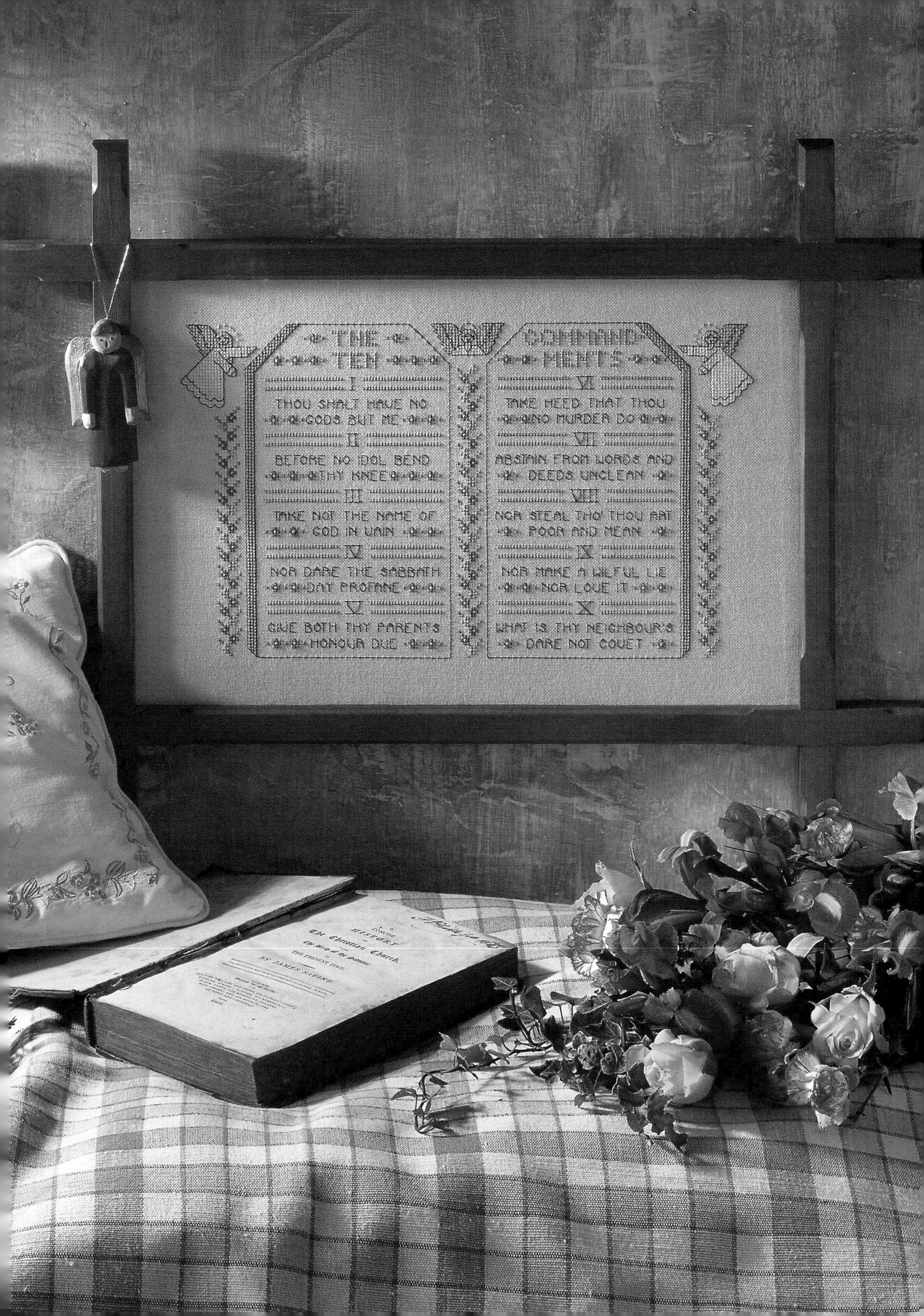

THE TEN
COMMAND-MENTS
I
THOU SHALT HAVE NO GODS BUT ME
II
BEFORE NO IDOL BEND THY KNEE
III
TAKE NOT THE NAME OF GOD IN VAIN
IV
NOR DARE THE SABBATH DAY PROFANE
V
GIVE BOTH THY PARENTS HONOUR DUE
VI
TAKE HEED THAT THOU NO MURDER DO
VII
ABSTAIN FROM WORDS AND DEEDS UNCLEAN
VIII
NOR STEAL THO' THOU ART POOR AND MEAN
IX
NOR MAKE A WILFUL LIE NOR LOVE IT
X
WHAT IS THY NEIGHBOUR'S DARE NOT COVET
HISTORY
The Christian Church
BY JAMES SABINE

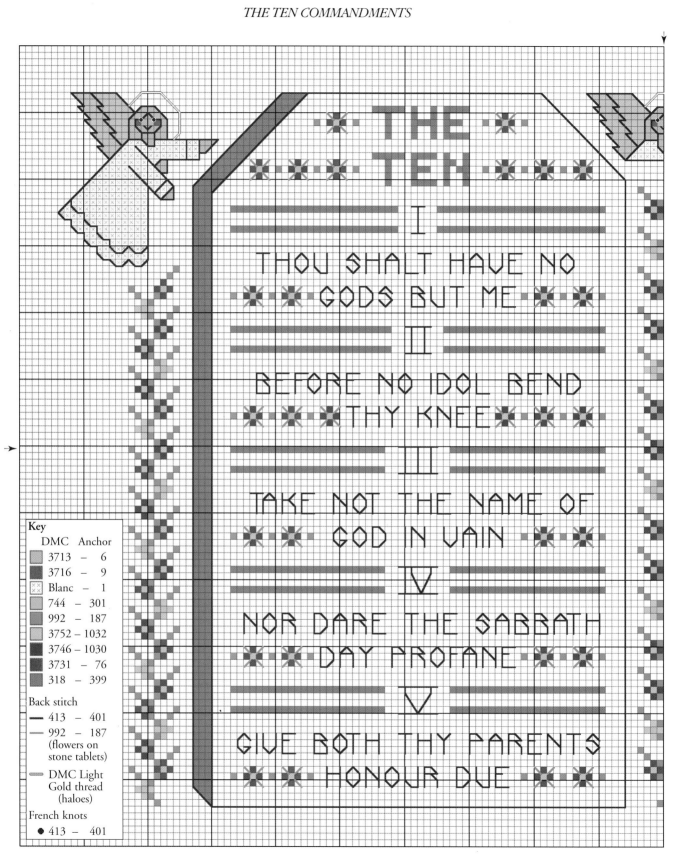

Key

DMC	Anchor
3713	6
3716	9
Blanc	1
744	301
992	187
3752	1032
3746	1030
3731	76
318	399

Back stitch

— 413 – 401

— 992 – 187
(flowers on stone tablets)

— DMC Light Gold thread (haloes)

French knots

● 413 – 401

THE TEN

I

THOU SHALT HAVE NO GODS BUT ME

II

BEFORE NO IDOL BEND THY KNEE

III

TAKE NOT THE NAME OF GOD IN VAIN

IV

NOR DARE THE SABBATH DAY PROFANE

V

GIVE BOTH THY PARENTS HONOUR DUE

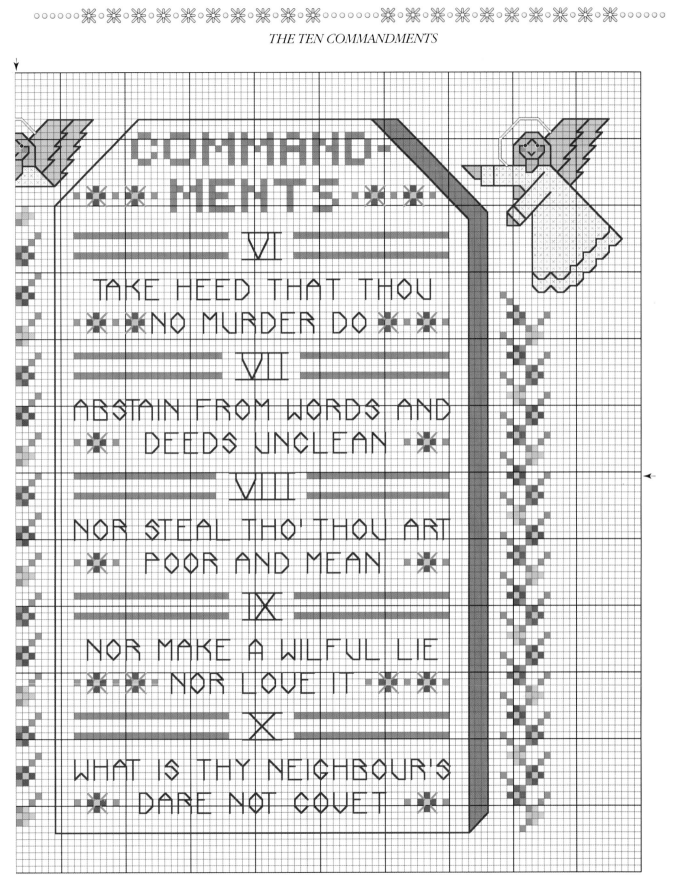

First Sewing Kit

Encourage a young stitcher to take up cross stitch with this first sewing kit.

NEEDLE CASE

FINISHED SIZE $4\frac{1}{4}$ x 3in (11 x 7.5cm)

YOU WILL NEED:
19 x 4in (48 x 10cm) 11 count Aida fabric, colour 264/cream
Stranded cottons (floss) as in the colour key
Tapestry needle, size 24
2 pieces white felt 8 x $2\frac{3}{4}$in (20 x 7cm)
Pinking shears
Cream sewing thread

Use 3 strands of stranded cotton (floss) for all cross stitches, and 2 strands for the back stitches.

1 Mark out the Aida fabric into sections (a), (b), (c) and (d) as illustrated in Fig 14, using tacking (basting) thread to mark the divisions.
2 Stitch the design centrally on part (c).
3 Right sides together, fold parts (a) and (b) over parts (c) and (d). Seam parts (a) and (d) together, allowing $\frac{1}{2}$in (1.5cm) for seams and leaving a 1in (2.5cm) gap in the middle.
4 Refold the fabric, right sides together, so that part (a) is lying directly over part (b), and part (d) is over part (c). Stitch the top and bottom seams (Fig 15), allowing $\frac{1}{2}$in (1.5cm) for seams.
5 Remove the tacking (basting) threads, turn right side out and slipstitch the gap closed.
6 Using pinking shears, cut 2 pieces of white felt 8 x $2\frac{3}{4}$in (20 x 7cm). Sew these inside the case, to hide the seam and form 4 leaves.

FIRST SEWING KIT

Key

DMC	Anchor		DMC	Anchor		DMC	Anchor		DMC	Anchor		DMC	Anchor
820	– 134		727	– 293		954	– 203		321	– 9046		Back stitch	
602	– 57		604	– 55		747	– 158		699	– 923		602	– 57
Blanc	– 1		813	– 161		726	– 295		740	– 316		Blanc	– 1

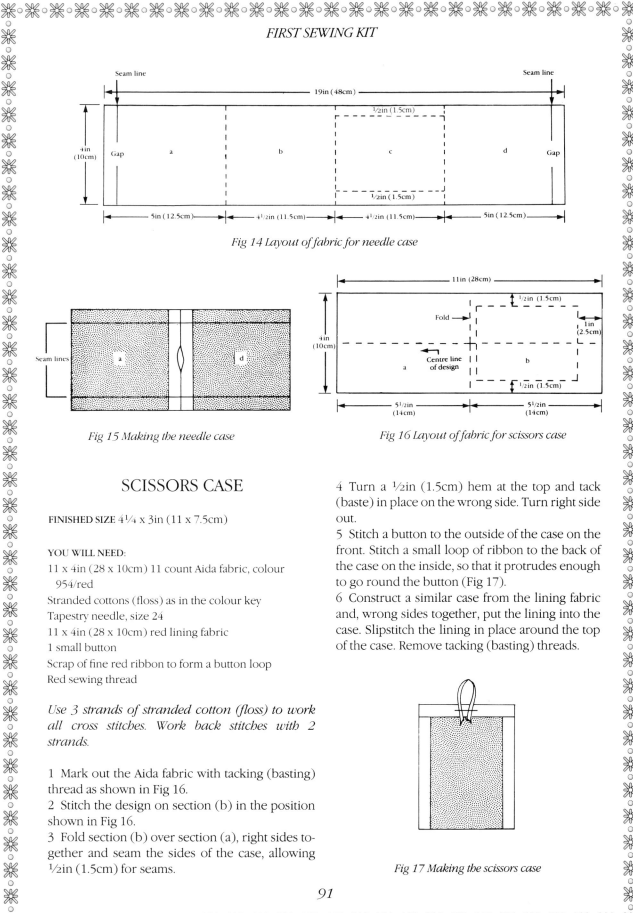

Fig 14 Layout of fabric for needle case

Fig 15 Making the needle case

Fig 16 Layout of fabric for scissors case

SCISSORS CASE

FINISHED SIZE $4^{1}/_{4}$ x 3in (11 x 7.5cm)

YOU WILL NEED:

11 x 4in (28 x 10cm) 11 count Aida fabric, colour
954/red
Stranded cottons (floss) as in the colour key
Tapestry needle, size 24
11 x 4in (28 x 10cm) red lining fabric
1 small button
Scrap of fine red ribbon to form a button loop
Red sewing thread

Use 3 strands of stranded cotton (floss) to work all cross stitches. Work back stitches with 2 strands.

1 Mark out the Aida fabric with tacking (basting) thread as shown in Fig 16.

2 Stitch the design on section (b) in the position shown in Fig 16.

3 Fold section (b) over section (a), right sides together and seam the sides of the case, allowing $^{1}/_{2}$in (1.5cm) for seams.

4 Turn a $^{1}/_{2}$in (1.5cm) hem at the top and tack (baste) in place on the wrong side. Turn right side out.

5 Stitch a button to the outside of the case on the front. Stitch a small loop of ribbon to the back of the case on the inside, so that it protrudes enough to go round the button (Fig 17).

6 Construct a similar case from the lining fabric and, wrong sides together, put the lining into the case. Slipstitch the lining in place around the top of the case. Remove tacking (basting) threads.

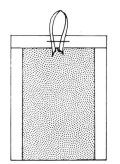

Fig 17 Making the scissors case

Doll's House Sampler

Worked on fine silk gauze, this sampler will grace the walls of any doll's house to delight the young householder. To stitch this sampler I had to wear two pairs of spectacles at once, which caused my daughters great amusement, so this project is for the eagle-eyed only.

FINISHED SIZE 1 x 1½in (2.5 x 4cm)

YOU WILL NEED:
One 4in (10cm) square 40-count silk gauze mounted in a card mat
Stranded cottons (floss) as in the colour key

Fine crewel needle
Doll's house picture frame 1 x 1½in (2.5 x 4cm)

Use 1 strand of stranded cotton (floss) for all cross and back stitches. Work all stitches over 1 thread of the gauze.

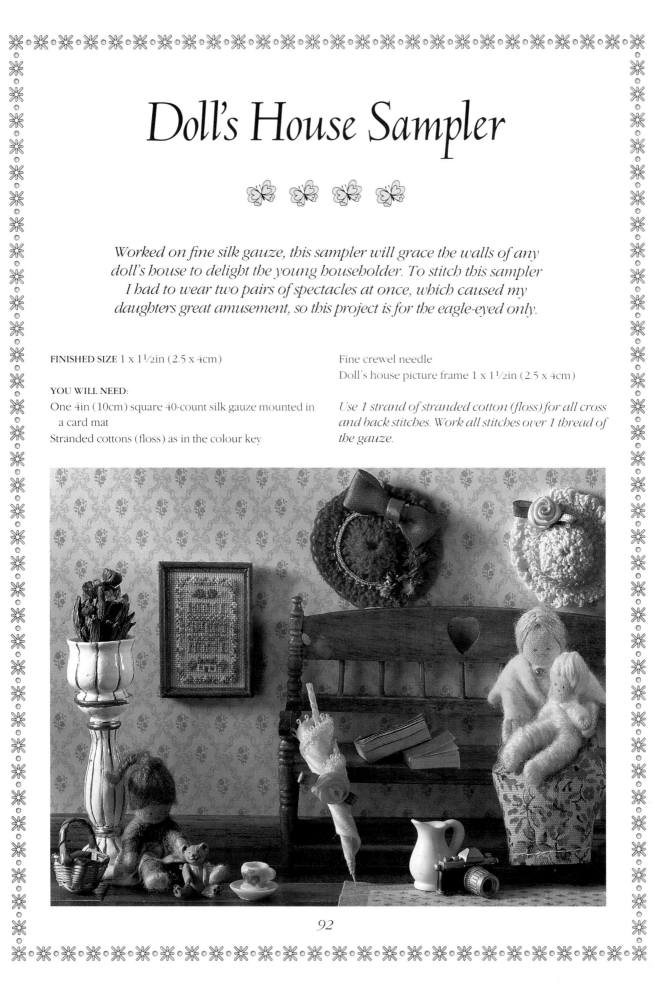

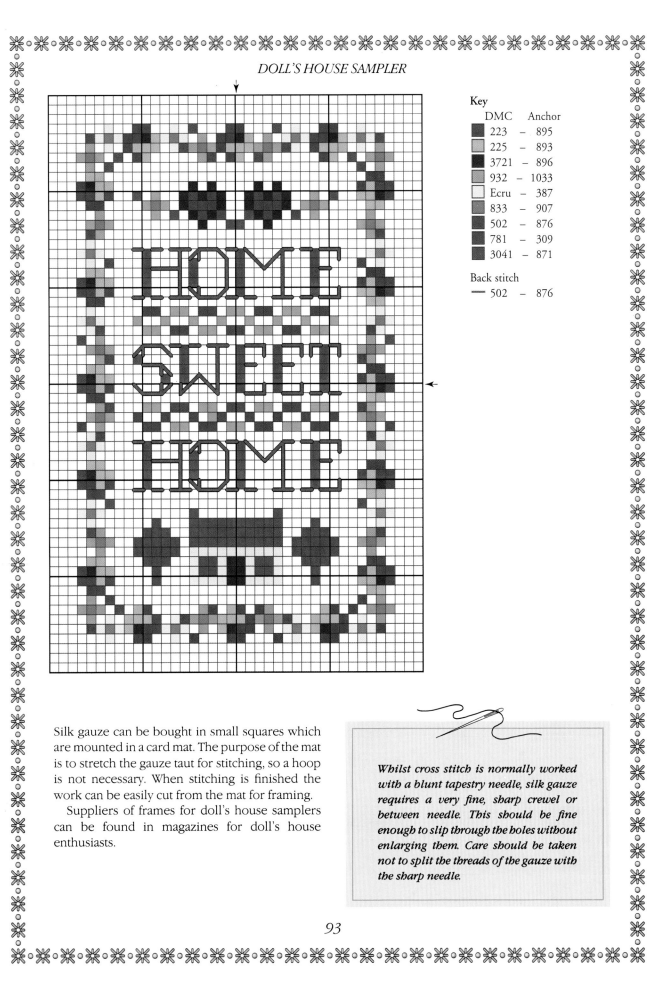

Key

DMC	Anchor
223	– 895
225	– 893
3721	– 896
932	– 1033
Ecru	– 387
833	– 907
502	– 876
781	– 309
3041	– 871

Back stitch
— 502 – 876

Silk gauze can be bought in small squares which are mounted in a card mat. The purpose of the mat is to stretch the gauze taut for stitching, so a hoop is not necessary. When stitching is finished the work can be easily cut from the mat for framing.

Suppliers of frames for doll's house samplers can be found in magazines for doll's house enthusiasts.

Whilst cross stitch is normally worked with a blunt tapestry needle, silk gauze requires a very fine, sharp crewel or between needle. This should be fine enough to slip through the holes without enlarging them. Care should be taken not to split the threads of the gauze with the sharp needle.

The Old Woman Who Lived in a Shoe

There was an old woman who lived in a shoe,
She had so many children she didn't
know what to do.
This lively interpretation of the nursery
rhyme will brighten the wall of any
youngster's room, and may also strike a
chord with all hard-pressed mothers.

FINISHED SIZE 7½ x 7½in (19 x 19cm)

YOU WILL NEED:
12 x 12in (31 x 31cm) Zweigart Linda fabric, colour
   264/ivory
Stranded cottons (floss) as in the colour key
Tapestry needle, size 26
Frame

Use 2 strands of stranded cotton (floss) to work all
cross stitches. Work back stitches and French knots
with 1 strand.

When the embroidery is complete, frame the
picture in the frame of your choice.

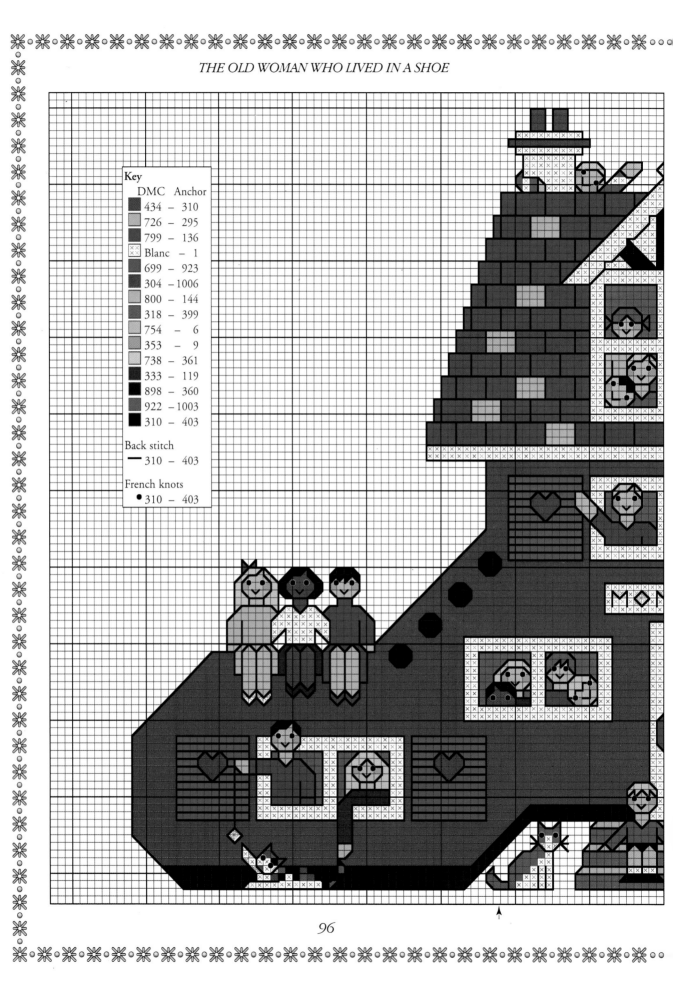

Key

	DMC	Anchor
	434	– 310
	726	– 295
	799	– 136
	Blanc	– 1
	699	– 923
	304	– 1006
	800	– 144
	318	– 399
	754	– 6
	353	– 9
	738	– 361
	333	– 119
	898	– 360
	922	– 1003
	310	– 403

Back stitch
— 310 – 403

French knots
● 310 – 403

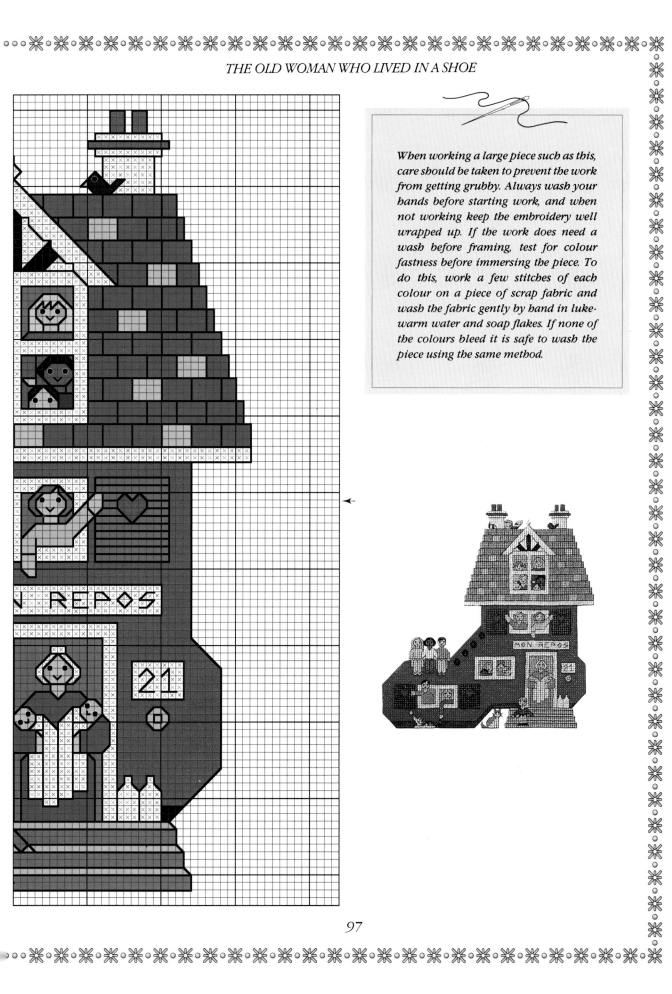

When working a large piece such as this, care should be taken to prevent the work from getting grubby. Always wash your hands before starting work, and when not working keep the embroidery well wrapped up. If the work does need a wash before framing, test for colour fastness before immersing the piece. To do this, work a few stitches of each colour on a piece of scrap fabric and wash the fabric gently by hand in luke-warm water and soap flakes. If none of the colours bleed it is safe to wash the piece using the same method.

Tinker, Tailor

Whom will I marry? Tinker, tailor, soldier, sailor, rich man, poor man, beggar man or thief? Traditionally children used this counting rhyme to count cherry stones onto the side of their pudding plates.

FINISHED SIZE 9 x 4in (23 x 10cm)

YOU WILL NEED:
16 x 12in (41 x 31cm) Zweigart Linda fabric, colour
   264/ivory
Stranded cottons (floss) as in the colour key
Tapestry needle, size 26
Frame

Use 2 strands of stranded cotton (floss) to work all cross stitches. Work back stitches and French knots with 1 strand.

When the embroidery is complete, frame the picture in the frame of your choice.

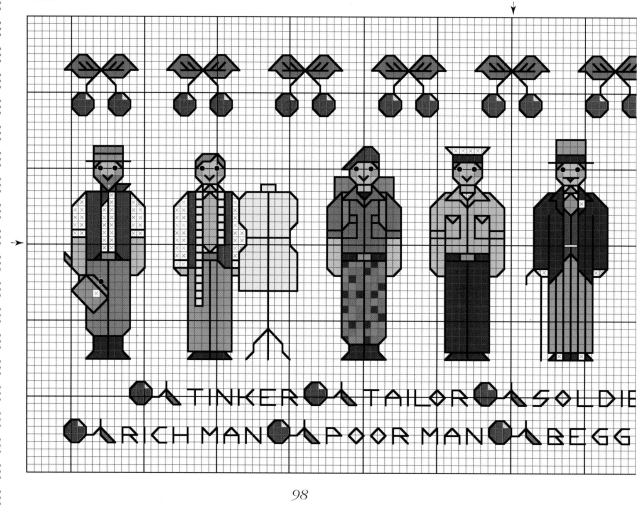

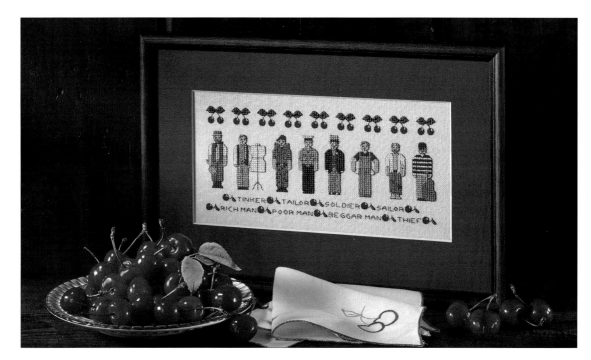

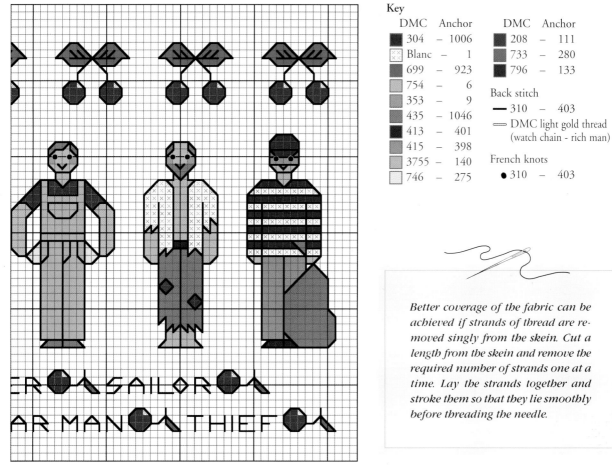

Key

DMC		Anchor	DMC		Anchor
304	–	1006	208	–	111
Blanc	–	1	733	–	280
699	–	923	796	–	133
754	–	6			
353	–	9			
435	–	1046			
413	–	401			
415	–	398			
3755	–	140			
746	–	275			

Back stitch
— 310 – 403
⟹ DMC light gold thread
 (watch chain - rich man)

French knots
● 310 – 403

Better coverage of the fabric can be achieved if strands of thread are removed singly from the skein. Cut a length from the skein and remove the required number of strands one at a time. Lay the strands together and stroke them so that they lie smoothly before threading the needle.

99

Noah's Ark

Children will not only enjoy looking at this picture, but will also enjoy helping Mr and Mrs Noah to load the pocket in the ark with the extra animals which are literally hanging about, waiting to go on board.

FINISHED SIZE 9½ x 6½in (24 x 16.5cm)

YOU WILL NEED:
Zweigart Linda fabric, colour 264/ivory
   15 x 12in (38 x 31cm) for the top of the ark
   15 x 7in (38 x 18cm) for the bottom of the ark
   6 pieces 4 x 4in (10 x 10cm) for the extra animals
   6 pieces 4 x 4in (10 x 10cm) to back the extra animals
Stranded cottons (floss) as in the colour key
Glissen Gloss Rainbow metallic thread, colour 116
Tapestry needle, size 26
Cream sewing thread
Scraps of stiff white card or 14-count plastic canvas
6 gold eyelet screws
6 gold jewellery jump rings

Use 2 strands of stranded cotton (floss) to work all cross stitches. Use 2 strands of Glissen Gloss to work the flood water. Work back stitches and French knots with 1 strand.

1 Work the top of the ark on the 15 x 12in (38 x 31cm) piece of fabric. Position the embroidery centrally, so that the top of the design is 3in (7.5cm) from the top of the fabric (Fig 18).
2 Work the bottom of the ark on the 15 x 7in (38 x 18cm) piece of fabric. Position the embroidery centrally, so that the top of the design is 1½in (4cm) from the top of the fabric (Fig 18, page 104).
3 Work each of the extra animals on the 4 x 4in (10 x 10cm) pieces of fabric.
4 To finish the bottom of the ark, turn the un-worked 1½in (4cm) of fabric at the top to the

Key

DMC	Anchor
762	234
519	1038
943	188
517	162
Blanc	1
437	362
413	401
433	371
938	381
3713	1020
310	403
318	399
746	275
304	1006
725	305
550	101
971	316

Back stitch
— 310 – 403
⇒ Glissen gloss 116
(flood water)

French knots
● 310 – 403

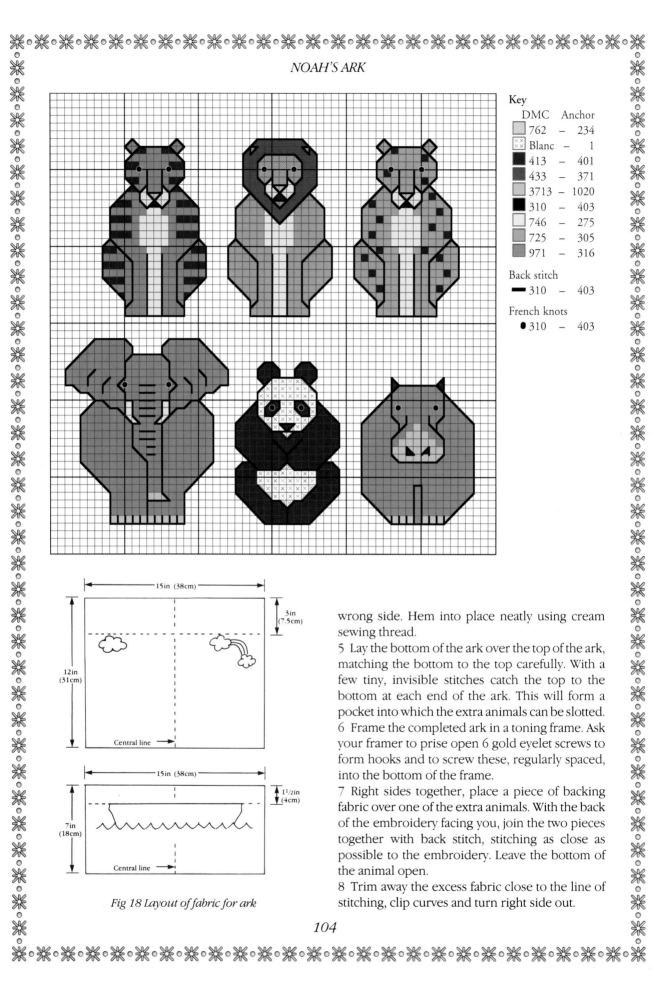

Key

DMC		Anchor
762	–	234
Blanc	–	1
413	–	401
433	–	371
3713	–	1020
310	–	403
746	–	275
725	–	305
971	–	316

Back stitch
— 310 – 403

French knots
● 310 – 403

15in (38cm)

3in (7.5cm)

12in (31cm)

Central line →

15in (38cm)

1½in (4cm)

7in (18cm)

Central line →

Fig 18 Layout of fabric for ark

wrong side. Hem into place neatly using cream sewing thread.

5 Lay the bottom of the ark over the top of the ark, matching the bottom to the top carefully. With a few tiny, invisible stitches catch the top to the bottom at each end of the ark. This will form a pocket into which the extra animals can be slotted.

6 Frame the completed ark in a toning frame. Ask your framer to prise open 6 gold eyelet screws to form hooks and to screw these, regularly spaced, into the bottom of the frame.

7 Right sides together, place a piece of backing fabric over one of the extra animals. With the back of the embroidery facing you, join the two pieces together with back stitch, stitching as close as possible to the embroidery. Leave the bottom of the animal open.

8 Trim away the excess fabric close to the line of stitching, clip curves and turn right side out.

9 Slip a small rectangle of white card into the animal to stiffen it and slipstitch the gap closed. Use plastic canvas instead of card if you want the animal to be washable.

10 Stitch a jewellery jump ring to the top of each extra animal's head and hang the animals from the hooks on the frame.

Metallic thread is used to work the flood water. As metallic thread can be prone to tangle, split and fray, use shorter lengths of thread than you would normally use.

Noah's Ark

Greetings Cards

BIRTHDAYS

For all youngsters, a birthday is the highlight of the year, so celebrate with a special card which is adaptable for any age. The trio of cards illustrated show the versatility of this simple but effective design.

FINISHED SIZE 3½ x 3½in (9 x 9cm)

YOU WILL NEED:
7 x 7in (18 x 18cm) 11 count Aida, colour 264/cream
Stranded cottons (floss) as in the colour key
Tapestry needle, size 24
Card mount with 4in (10cm) diameter circular window
Gold or silver plastic 15mm numbers
UHU glue
Trimmings of your choice

Use 3 strands of stranded cotton (floss) to work all cross stitches. Use 2 strands to work the lettering. Work the antennae and outline the butterflies with 1 strand.

When the stitching is complete, mount the embroidery into a card following the instructions on page 117. Glue the required numbers to the centre of the design and trim the card with lace or ribbons.

Double-sided sticky tape allows you to peel the work off and reposition it until you are happy that it is straight and evenly spaced in the centre of the window.

Key		(pink version)		(mauve version)	
	DMC Anchor		DMC Anchor		DMC Anchor
■	407 – 914	–	407 – 914	–	407 – 914
■	798 – 131	–	600 – 78	–	333 – 119
■	809 – 130	–	605 – 74	–	340 – 118
■	600 – 78	–	782 – 308	–	600 – 78
■	603 – 76	–	725 – 306	–	603 – 76
■	605 – 74	–	727 – 293	–	605 – 74
■	340 – 118	–	809 – 130	–	809 – 130
☐	727 – 293	–	727 – 293	–	727 – 293
■	992 – 187	–	992 – 187	–	992 – 187

Back stitch

—	798 – 131	–	600 – 78	–	333 – 119
—	407 – 914	–	407 – 914	–	407 – 914
					(antennae)

FIRST COMMUNION OR CONFIRMATION

This is a mix-and-match design which serves for both boys and girls and both sacraments. Choose whether you want a boy or a girl kneeling at the altar rail, and choose the symbol for either communion or confirmation.

Use 2 strands of stranded cotton (floss) to work all cross stitches. Work back stitches and French knots with 1 strand.

FINISHED SIZE 2 x 4in (5 x 10cm)

YOU WILL NEED:
6 x 9in (15 x 23cm) Zweigart Linda fabric, colour
  264/ivory
Stranded cottons (floss) as in the colour key
Tapestry needle, size 26
Church window style card mount with a 5½in (14cm)
  window

1 Depending on the circumstances, embroider either a boy or a girl at the bottom of the design; both are charted for you and are interchangeable. At the top of the design, stitch either the chalice and host for a first communion, or stitch the jar of chrism for a confirmation. Add a name, a date and the event, using the alphabet and numbers provided.
2 When the stitching is complete, mount the embroidery into a card following the instructions on page 117.

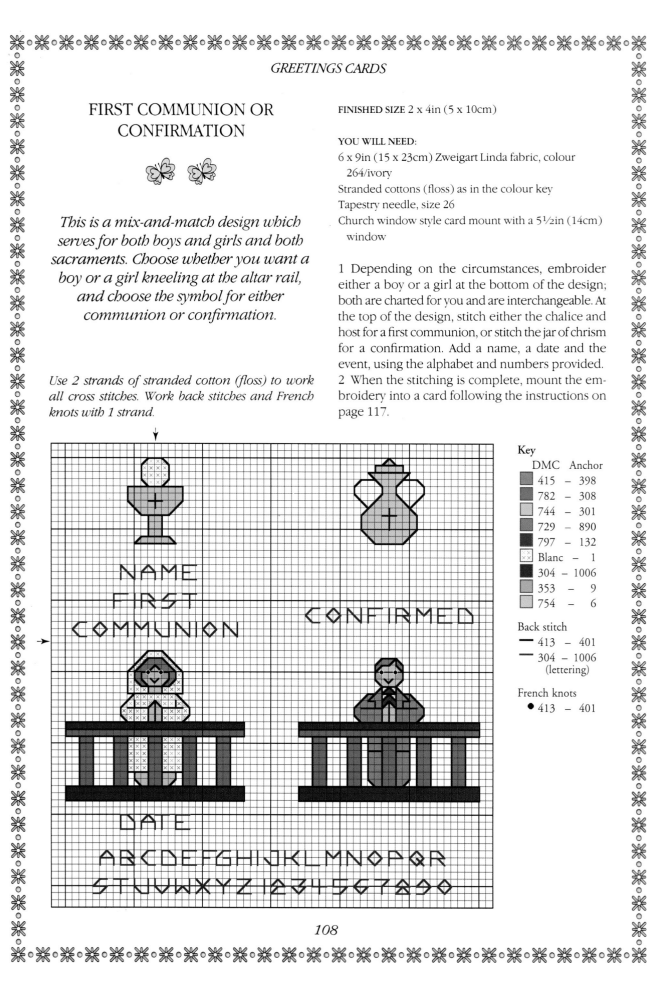

Key

DMC	Anchor
415	– 398
782	– 308
744	– 301
729	– 890
797	– 132
Blanc	– 1
304	– 1006
353	– 9
754	– 6

Back stitch
— 413 – 401
— 304 – 1006
   (lettering)

French knots
● 413 – 401

BADEN-POWELL AWARD

Both my daughters were Girl Guides and both gained their Baden-Powell awards. This design is based on the badges which were presented to them and can be used to congratulate a Girl Guide on a significant achievement.

FINISHED SIZE 3½ x 3½in (9 x 9cm)

YOU WILL NEED:
7 x 7in (18 x 18cm) Zweigart Linda fabric, colour 264/ivory
Stranded cottons (floss) as in the colour key
Tapestry needle, size 26
Card mount with 4in (10cm) diameter circular window

Use 2 strands of stranded cotton (floss) to work all cross stitches. Work back stitches with 1 strand.

When the stitching is complete, mount the embroidery into a card following the instructions on page 117.

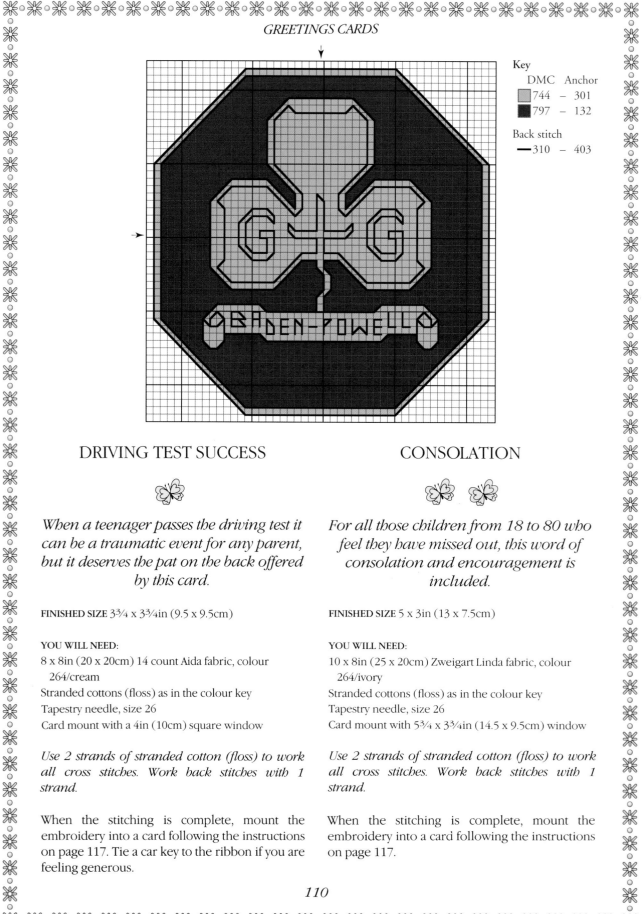

Key

	DMC	Anchor
▧	744	– 301
■	797	– 132

Back stitch
— 310 – 403

DRIVING TEST SUCCESS

When a teenager passes the driving test it can be a traumatic event for any parent, but it deserves the pat on the back offered by this card.

FINISHED SIZE 3¾ x 3¾in (9.5 x 9.5cm)

YOU WILL NEED:
8 x 8in (20 x 20cm) 14 count Aida fabric, colour 264/cream
Stranded cottons (floss) as in the colour key
Tapestry needle, size 26
Card mount with a 4in (10cm) square window

Use 2 strands of stranded cotton (floss) to work all cross stitches. Work back stitches with 1 strand.

When the stitching is complete, mount the embroidery into a card following the instructions on page 117. Tie a car key to the ribbon if you are feeling generous.

CONSOLATION

For all those children from 18 to 80 who feel they have missed out, this word of consolation and encouragement is included.

FINISHED SIZE 5 x 3in (13 x 7.5cm)

YOU WILL NEED:
10 x 8in (25 x 20cm) Zweigart Linda fabric, colour 264/ivory
Stranded cottons (floss) as in the colour key
Tapestry needle, size 26
Card mount with 5¾ x 3¾in (14.5 x 9.5cm) window

Use 2 strands of stranded cotton (floss) to work all cross stitches. Work back stitches with 1 strand.

When the stitching is complete, mount the embroidery into a card following the instructions on page 117.

Key

DMC Anchor
- 797 – 132
- Blanc – 1
- 304 – 1006
- 414 – 235

Back stitch
— 310 – 403

Key

DMC Anchor
- 801 – 359
- 782 – 308
- 797 – 132
- Blanc – 1
- 353 – 9
- 310 – 403

Back stitch
— 310 – 403
— 304 – 1006
(lettering)

WELL DONE

IT IS NEVER TOO LATE TO HAVE A HAPPY CHILDHOOD

Eighteenth Birthday Display Case

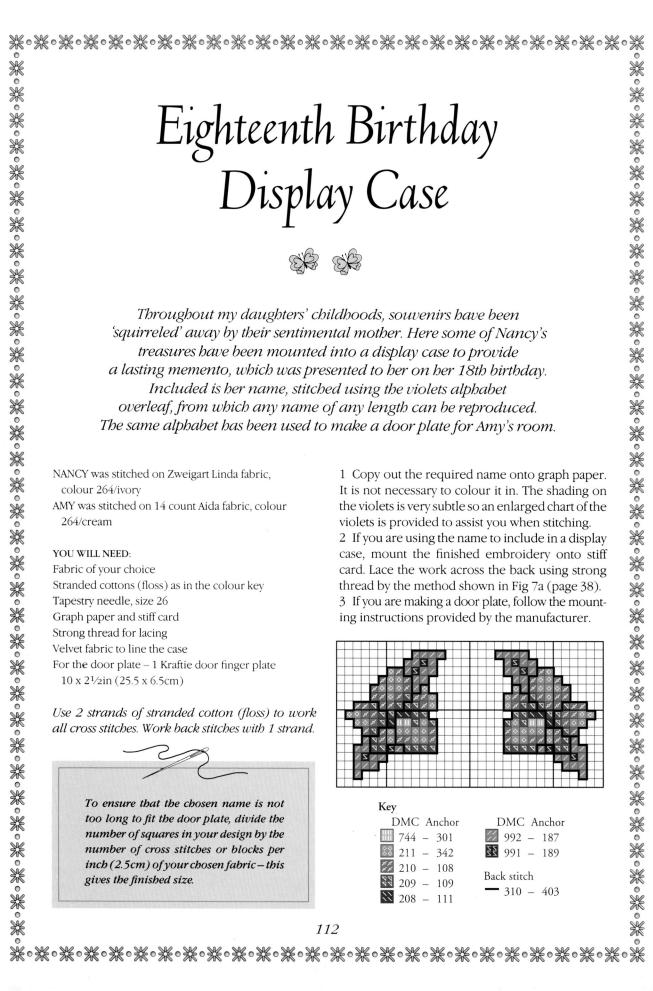

*Throughout my daughters' childhoods, souvenirs have been
'squirreled' away by their sentimental mother. Here some of Nancy's
treasures have been mounted into a display case to provide
a lasting memento, which was presented to her on her 18th birthday.
Included is her name, stitched using the violets alphabet
overleaf, from which any name of any length can be reproduced.
The same alphabet has been used to make a door plate for Amy's room.*

NANCY was stitched on Zweigart Linda fabric,
  colour 264/ivory
AMY was stitched on 14 count Aida fabric, colour
  264/cream

YOU WILL NEED:
Fabric of your choice
Stranded cottons (floss) as in the colour key
Tapestry needle, size 26
Graph paper and stiff card
Strong thread for lacing
Velvet fabric to line the case
For the door plate – 1 Kraftie door finger plate
  10 x 2½in (25.5 x 6.5cm)

*Use 2 strands of stranded cotton (floss) to work
all cross stitches. Work back stitches with 1 strand.*

**To ensure that the chosen name is not
too long to fit the door plate, divide the
number of squares in your design by the
number of cross stitches or blocks per
inch (2.5cm) of your chosen fabric – this
gives the finished size.**

1 Copy out the required name onto graph paper.
It is not necessary to colour it in. The shading on
the violets is very subtle so an enlarged chart of the
violets is provided to assist you when stitching.
2 If you are using the name to include in a display
case, mount the finished embroidery onto stiff
card. Lace the work across the back using strong
thread by the method shown in Fig 7a (page 38).
3 If you are making a door plate, follow the mounting instructions provided by the manufacturer.

Key

DMC	Anchor		DMC	Anchor
744	– 301		992	– 187
211	– 342		991	– 189
210	– 108			
209	– 109		Back stitch	
208	– 111		310	– 403

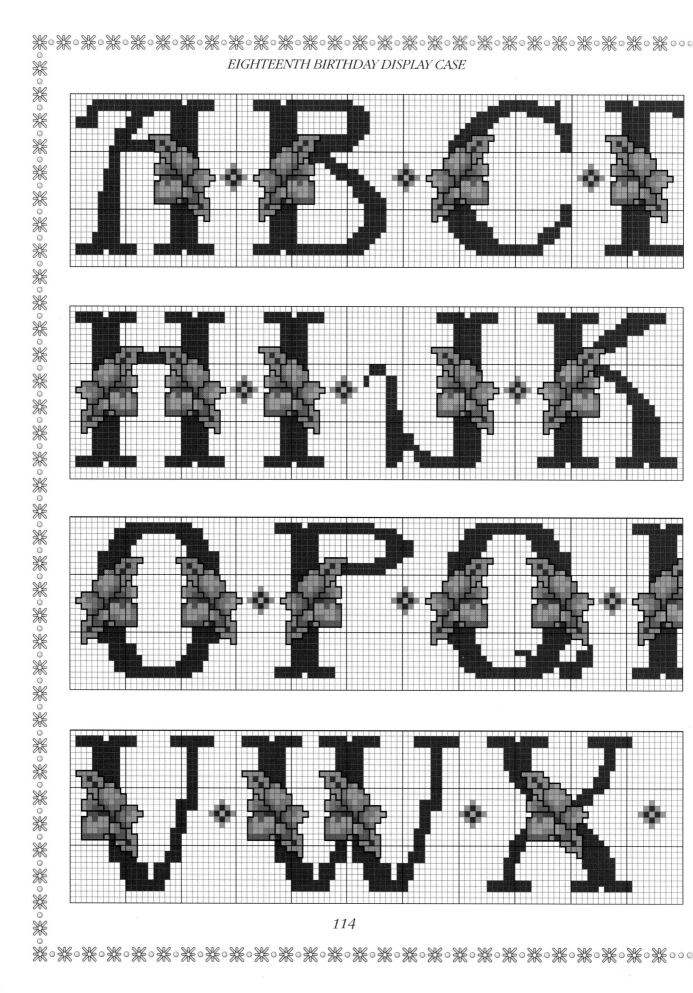

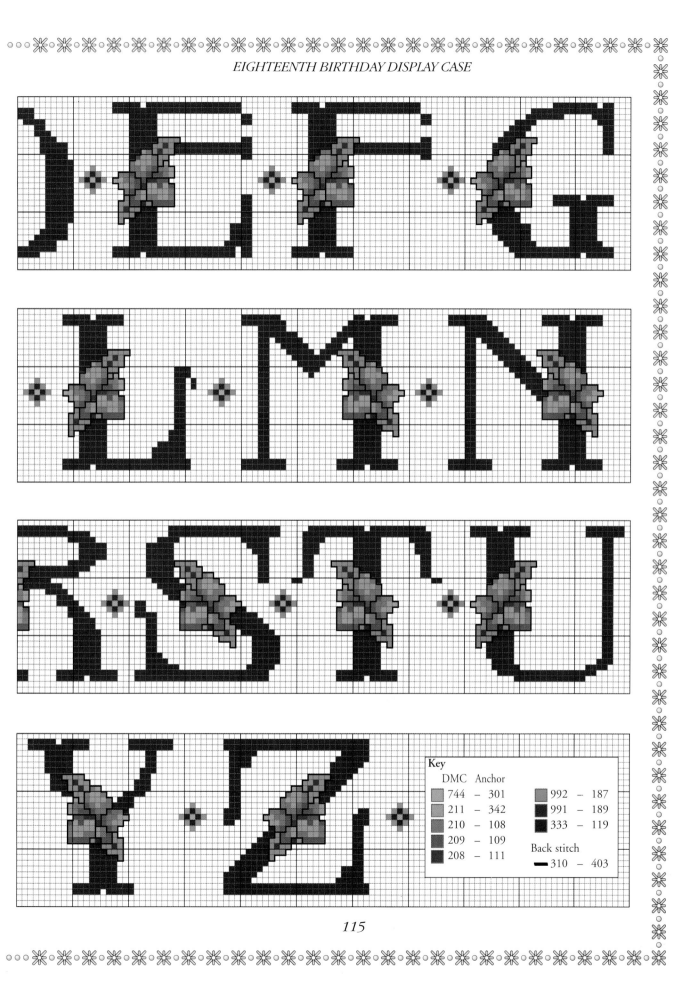

Key

DMC		Anchor
744	–	301
211	–	342
210	–	108
209	–	109
208	–	111
992	–	187
991	–	189
333	–	119

Back stitch
— 310 – 403

Basic Techniques

PREPARING THE FABRIC

Always neaten the edges of embroidery fabric before mounting it into a hoop or onto a frame, to avoid fraying.

Find the centre of your fabric by folding it in four, and mark this point temporarily with a pin. The centre of the design will be stitched at this point, unless the instructions say otherwise.

Each project tells you which fabric to use to get a result similar to the samples in the photographs. The finished size given with each project refers to the finished size of the embroidered design, not the framed or finished article. If you work on a different fabric the finished size may not be the same and mounting instructions may have to be adapted accordingly.

The size of fabric to cut is given as a minimum measurement. If mounting the fabric into a hoop (Fig 19) or onto a frame (Fig 20) for stitching, which is recommended, you might need to cut a larger piece to allow for this.

Small pieces of fabric can be mounted into hoops or onto frames if extra waste fabric is stitched to them first. Lay your embroidery fabric centrally on a piece of waste cotton fabric which will fit your hoop or frame (I use pieces of worn-out pillow cases). Stitch the two pieces

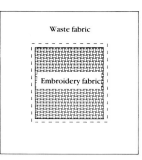

Fig 21 Adding waste fabric

of fabric together around the edge of the embroidery fabric and cut away the cotton fabric on the reverse exposing the back of the embroidery fabric (Fig 21). Mount the fabric into a hoop or onto a frame. When work is complete cut away the waste fabric.

STITCHES

A full square on the chart indicates the use of a full cross stitch, a right-angled triangle indicates a three-quarter cross stitch, a solid line indicates back stitch and a dot indicates a French knot.

Where white thread is used within a design it will appear in the colour key, otherwise leave empty squares on the graph as bare fabric.

FULL CROSS STITCH

A full cross stitch is worked over 2 threads on Linda fabric (Fig 22) and over one block on Aida (Fig 23).

When working rows of full cross stitches, bring the needle out at the left-hand side of the row and work a row of half crosses. Return, making the complete crosses, working from right to left and using the same holes as before. All stitches 'hold hands' sharing holes with their neighbours (Fig 24), unless they are single stitches worked on their own. Ensure that all top stitches are lying in the same direction.

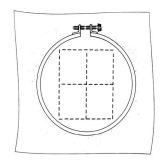

Fig 19 Mounting fabric into a hoop

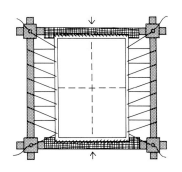

Fig 20 Mounting fabric onto a frame

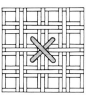

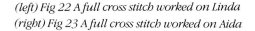

(left) Fig 22 A full cross stitch worked on Linda
(right) Fig 23 A full cross stitch worked on Aida

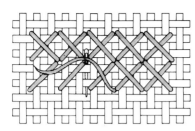

Fig 24 Working lines of full cross stitches

THREE-QUARTER CROSS STITCH

The first half of the cross stitch is formed in the usual way but the second 'quarter' stitch is brought across and down into the central hole (Fig 25).

Where the chart indicates two three-quarter stitches, these are worked sharing the same central hole and occupying the space of one full cross stitch (Fig 26).

(left) Fig 25 Four examples of three-quarter cross stitches
(right) Fig 26 Two three-quarter cross stitches sewn back to back in the space of one full cross stitch

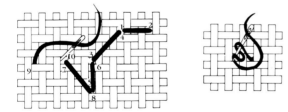

(left) Fig 27 Back stitch
(right) Fig 28 Working a French knot

BACK STITCH

Back stitch is worked around and sometimes over the completed cross stitch. It is also used for lettering. Bring the needle out at 1 and in again at 2. Bring it out again at 3 and in again at 4. Continue this sequence in the direction indicated by the chart (Fig 27).

FRENCH KNOTS

Bring the needle out one thread to the right of where you want the knot to lie. Slip the needle twice under the thread so that the twists lie snugly around the needle. Without allowing the thread to untwist, insert the needle back into the fabric one thread to the left of

where you started and pull the thread through to the back (Fig 28).

PRESSING YOUR EMBROIDERY

When all the stitching is complete, press your embroidery to remove any creases. To avoid flattening the stitches lay several layers of fluffy, white terry towel on a flat surface and place your work face down on the towel. Then cover the work with a thin cloth and press gently with a warm iron.

MOUNTING EMBROIDERY INTO A CARD

YOU WILL NEED:
Your finished embroidery
A ready-made card mount
Scissors
Double-sided sticky tape
Spray Mount adhesive
A large empty cardboard box
A sheet of scrap paper

A ready-made card mount will have three sections and a window already cut in it (Fig 29). Lay your embroidery on section (b) and trim the embroidery so that it is 1in (2.5cm) larger than the window. On the inside of the card, stick strips of double-sided sticky tape around the window and on section (a) as shown in Fig 29. For cards with square or rectangular windows stick four strips of the tape around the window.

The speckled area on section (a) indicates a squirt of Spray Mount adhesive. This is sprayed on to give the embroidery a sticky surface to cling to; without it the embroidery has a tendency to ripple. Place the card with the inside facing you in an upturned box. Mask sections (b) and (c) with a piece of scrap paper. Apply the Spray Mount to section (a). The box and paper will stop the adhesive going where it is not wanted.

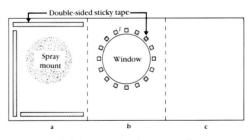

Fig 29 Mounting into a card

Next, lay your embroidery face up on a flat surface. Remove the backing strips from the sticky tape on the card. With the outside of the card facing you, stick the window around the embroidery, making sure that it is straight. You may need several tries, but persevere until you are satisfied. Turn the card over and stick section (a) over section (b), smoothing the embroidery down onto the Spray Mount. Trim with lace (glued in place using UHU), or tie on some ribbon, as a final touch.

Templates

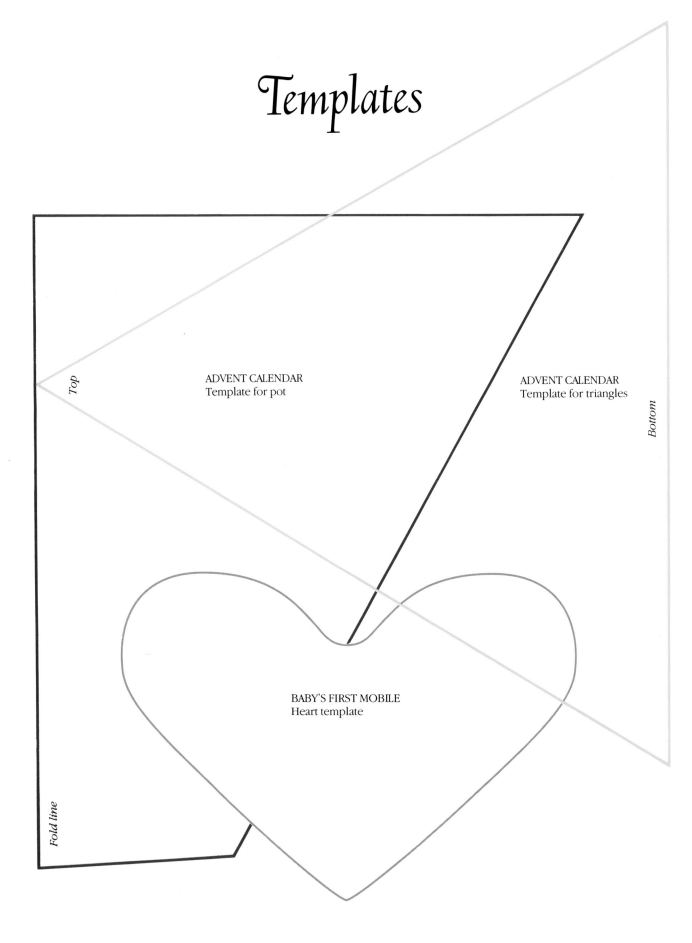

Top

Bottom

ADVENT CALENDAR
Template for pot

ADVENT CALENDAR
Template for triangles

BABY'S FIRST MOBILE
Heart template

Fold line

Suppliers

I am grateful to the following suppliers for their generous assistance in the production of this book:

Cara Ackerman and Maria Diaz at DMC Creative World Ltd, Pullman Road, Wigston, Leicestershire LE8 2DY, tel (0533) 811040 (Zweigart and Aida fabrics, DMC stranded cottons (floss), DMC Coton Retors Mat, DMC Flower threads)

Julie Gill at Coats Patons Crafts, McMullen Road, Darlington, Co Durham DL1 1YQ, tel (0325) 381010 (Anchor stranded cottons (floss))

Jenny Kearley at Craft Creations, Units 1–10 Harpers Yard, Ruskin Road, Tottenham, London N17 8NE, tel (081) 8852655 (all card mounts)

Ian Lawson-Smith at IL-Soft, 5, 6 & 7 Spinner's Court, West End, Witney, Oxon OX8 6NJ, tel (0993) 779274 (Cross Stitch Designer computer program)

Tony and Wendy Foster at Warwick Studios, 206–208 Emscote Road, Warwick CV34 5QT, tel (0926) 494714 (framers par excellence)

Mike Gray at Framecraft Miniatures Ltd, 372–376 Summer Lane, Hockley, Birmingham B19 3QA, tel (021) 212 0551 (silk gauze and bellpull ends)

Judy Raine at Janet Coles Beads Ltd, Perdiswell Cottage, Bilford Road, Worcester WR3 8QA, tel (0905) 755888 (beads for mobile and jewellery jump rings for ark)

Christine Springett at Springetts, 21 Hillmorton Road, Rugby, Warks CV22 5DF, tel (0788) 544691 (plastic numbers for birthday cards)

Simon Laycock at Craft Basics, 9 Gillygate, York YO3 7EA, tel (0904) 652840 (wooden hoop for mobile, curtain rings and jingle bells)

Sheila Mason at my excellent local needlecraft shop, Stitchcraft, 10 Whiteheads Court, Royal Priors, Leamington Spa CV32 4YA, tel (0926) 429013 (silk gauze, needlework supplies)

Voirrey Branthwaite at The Voirrey Embroidery Centre, Brimstage Hall, Brimstage, Wirrall L63 6JA, tel (051) 3423514 (needlework supplies)

Beryl Lee at Artisan, 19–21 High Street, Pinner, Middlesex HA5 5PJ, tel (081) 8660327 (needlework supplies and plastic canvas)

Gillian Leeper at Spoilt for Choice, 35 March Road, Wimblington, March, Cambs PE15 0RW, tel (0354) 740341 (Beadesign beads)

Dorothy Anne, 1A Mill Bridge, Skipton, North Yorkshire BD23 1NJ, tel (0756) 799894 (broderie anglaise lace, ref BA6954 for pin pillow)

Les Coombes at Pizienwell Arts, Wheatsheaf, Pizien Well Road, Wateringbury, Kent ME18 5HX, tel (0622) 812412 (Oxford frame)

Harry Wardlaw at the Sewing Basket, 4 Edinburgh Road, Formby, Liverpool L37 6EP, tel (0704) 873301 (Kraftie door finger plate)

C.M. Offray & Son Ltd, Fir Tree Place, Church Road, Ashford, Middlesex TW15 2PH, tel (0784) 247281 (ribbon)

When contacting suppliers through the post for catalogues or other information, please always enclose a SAE. If you telephone them, they will be able to tell you if there is a charge for their catalogue or price list.

ACKNOWLEDGEMENTS

I cannot thank enough the team of expert needlewomen who, yet again, came to my rescue with the stitching of the projects. Without their skill and willingness to give of their time so generously, this book would have been at least another year in the making.

A huge thank you, therefore, to Win Barry (page 41), Gill Broad (page 63), Carol Burr (page 101), Eileen Callender (page 99), Hazel Evans (page 17), Ros Foster (page 9), Margaret Jones (page 49), Sandra Kedzlie (page 67), Elizabeth Lovesey (pages 26–7), Edna McCready (page 17), Sue Moir (page 29), Sue Moore (pages 26–7), Sylvia Morgan (pages 6, 81), Val Morgan (pages 41, 70, 75, 113), Penny Peberdy (page 95), Ann Sansom (page 109), Elizabeth Smith (page 113), Linda Smith (pages 13, 89), Christine Thomas (page 35), Amy Verso (page 107), Nancy Verso (pages 107, 109), Irene Vincent (page 85), and Jenny Way (page 53).

Many thanks to Vivienne Wells, Brenda Morrison and Sue Rhodes at David & Charles for their invaluable help, to Joanna Gormley for her efforts, to Tony Fuller who nursed me through the tricky bits, and to Donna Ashbaugh, Faye Smelich, Carla and Jim Tate for their assistance in the 'foraging for supplies' department.

Many thanks also to Ian Lawson-Smith for his support during my first steps into computer designed charts, and to Ethan Danielson who edited the charts with such patience.

For the delectable photographs I am indebted to Tim and Zöe Hill.

Index

Page numbers in *italics* indicate illustrations